Hours of Power

Hours of Power

—◇—

*My Daily Book of Motivation
and Inspiration*

—◇—

Robert H. Schuller

HarperSanFrancisco
A Division of HarperCollins*Publishers*

HarperCollins books may be purchased for educational, business, or sales promotional use. For information please write: Special Markets Department, HarperCollins Publishers, Inc., 10 East 53rd Street, New York, NY 10022.

HarperCollins Web site: http://www.harpercollins.com
HarperCollins®, ▰®, and HarperSanFrancisco™ are trademarks of
HarperCollins Publishers, Inc.

FIRST EDITION

Library of Congress Cataloging-in-Publication Data
available upon request.

ISBN 0-06-072706-3 (cloth)

04 05 06 07 08 RRD(H) 10 9 8 7 6 5 4 3 2 1

The Possibility Thinker's Creed

When faced with a mountain,
I will not quit!
I will keep on striving
until I climb over,
find a pass through,
tunnel underneath,
or simply stay and turn
the mountain into a gold mine—
with God's help!

Contents

Born for Eternity

There was a Western farmer who on a mountain hike found an egg lying in the grass. He picked it up, took it home, and put it under the hen that was sitting on chicken eggs. Eventually the hen hatched the egg along with the other eggs. But what came forth was the most awkward, crude, ugly-looking creature the farmer ever saw. He called the neighbors in and asked if they knew what it was but they could not tell. Nobody had the slightest idea what this peculiar creature was. It developed wings that became a heavy burden on the little body—big, oversized, clumsy wings that were too big for him. And its legs developed deformed crooks that looked like claws, and the beak, instead of being straight and sharp, was crooked. It survived and it grew until one day, above the barnyard, there was a shrill scream and this awkward bird looked up and he saw gliding slowly in great circles above the farmyard a huge bird; and for the first time, his instinct told him what he was. He was an eagle—bred for the mountains, born to fly, and destined never to be happy while earthbound in a barnyard.

Ah, that's it. Why do human beings have such frustrations, such disturbances, such mental problems? We may have legs and we may have mouths and we may have eyes like animals. But we are bred for heaven. And so, St. Augustine said, "No human being is really at peace until he has come to God by faith." We instinctively feel the call of eternity, like the wild, domesticated animal who hears the call of the wild and must respond. One wise philosopher said that when God wants to prove something to people He puts it in their instincts. So that is Christ's first word on the subject; we are born for eternity.

◆

For Spiritual Awareness

Too often, O God, the sacred calm of your still small voice is overpowered by the roar of the traffic, the moan of ambulances, the wail of sirens, the growl of buses, the rude interruption of the doorbell. Jet airplanes, trucks, trains, television, telephones fill my everyday world with noises my ears were never designed to tolerate.

An irritating assortment of unnatural sounds drowns your silver-soft voice, Lord, which whispers through the trees. Oh, my Lord, there are birds winging and I do not see them, children playing and I do not hear them, flowers blooming and I do not enjoy them, clouds sailing silently through the soundless sea of space and I do not see them!

God, you are living and moving and I do not feel you! Increase my awareness of the throbbing reality of the dynamic, spiritual universe around me, Lord. God! You are moving in mighty thoughts and feelings within me now! I am surrounded with an awareness of you that gives me a new lease on life!

Thank you, God. Amen.

—◆—

The Valley of the Shadow

Real relief from tension and nervousness comes to the person who feels the presence of God. Peace of mind comes to the person who feels the presence of God.

No one has put it better than the Psalmist: "Yea, though I walk through the valley of the shadow of death, I will fear no evil: for thou art with me." This simple sentence has calmed more nervous souls, comforted more lonely people, encouraged more timid hearts than all the tranquilizers and psychiatrists put together!

Nothing can stop the man who feels the presence of God in his life. Terror is like morning dew in a noonday sun. Fear is ice on summer seas. The tense, trembling, troubled heart becomes as placid and peaceful as water in an inland lake moments before the dawning of the day.

—◇—

Trouble Feeling God's Presence?

But there are some people who do not seem to feel God's presence at all. Why? Perhaps the major reason is the fact that they do not want to feel God's presence. They don't experience it because they don't want to. St. John said, "They love darkness rather than light because their deeds are evil." The little boy who is up to mischief doesn't want his daddy to come around. And the housewife whose house is disorderly and unclean does not want company.

This explains why some people never go to church, or read their Bible, and, in fact, deliberately avoid Christian people, lest they expose their own lives to judgment! The way an overweight person avoids stepping on the bathroom scales, or the way an untidy person avoids looking in the mirror, or the way someone who has neglected his teeth avoids the dentist, or someone who hasn't paid his bills avoids the mailbox—so some people are perfectly content not to have God come around!

Do you know how God punishes us for this? By giving us exactly what we want: He leaves us alone! And that's the beginning of hell on earth!

But how about good people who have trouble feeling God's presence? For many, I suspect, the world gets in the way. Brains become barriers. Eyes and ears become obstacles. The blind ploughman wrote, "God took away my eyes that my soul might see!" There is good reason why men close their eyes when they pray! "The world knoweth him not, for it seeth him not; but ye know him, for he dwells in you," was Christ's word on this point.

—◇—

Keep Your Faith Fresh

How do you explain religious people who have trouble feeling God's presence? What is their problem? Who knows? Perhaps God deliberately limits His revelation in order to keep us from becoming "so heavenly minded that we are no earthly good." . . . One reason is that some people keep trying to ride along through life on an old religious experience. This just does not work. The great Christian experience you had cannot last long before it will have lost its luster.

The sanctuary of the Garden Grove Community Church is a hundred and forty feet long. The walls are entirely made of glass. Slowly, suddenly, the clearness of the glass becomes clouded through a collected film that adheres to the glass bit by bit until the sunshine no longer shines through, sparkling and golden. The windows need to be washed. The film needs to be cleansed away. Life has a way of putting a film over our old religious experiences until we can no longer see God clearly. We need a new experience with Him! One small group of Christian people that meets regularly always makes this announcement before every meeting: "What new experience have you had with God this past week? We don't want to hear your old stories!"

For Thou Art with Me

There may be times when you do not feel God's presence. For a moment you may be almost terrified at His apparent absence. But when your life is at its worst, God will meet you in the blackest moments, and you will grow strangely quiet and peaceful, knowing that you are not walking alone.

That great Scottish preacher, John McNeill, related how as a young lad he worked late on Saturdays. To reach home he would have to walk through seven dark, dangerous miles on a road that was infamous for robbers and thieves. "One Saturday it was past midnight before I finished my work and left for home. Two miles out of town the road got blacker than ever. There were high, wooded hills on the right and high, wooded hills on the left. The night was as black as a wolf's jaw. I was sixteen years old. I was moving along so fast that my feet hardly touched the ground. Then, suddenly, twenty yards in front of me, so it seemed, there rang out a great, strong, manly voice. 'Is that you, Johnny?' And for a moment I couldn't really have told you my name! And then I recovered. That was my father come to meet me at the worst of it! His voice first startled me and then delivered me from all my fears. The night became light around me! His hand on my shoulder, his voice in my ear, and his feet rising, falling on the road beside my own, I feared no evil, for he was with me. I can't tell you any more about the road home that night. Why? Because I was as good as home right there. All that makes home home was with me!" "Yea, though I walk through the valley of the shadow of death, I will fear no evil; for thou art with me."

——◆——

You Are Mine

Where is God when we can't feel His presence? He is in people. Trust Him! He sends people who affirm their love to you. Yes, people you never knew before. Have you experienced the loss of a loved one, a father, a mother, a child, a spouse? Did you receive a medical report that you have cancer? Have you had a breast amputated, or have you picked up a terminal disease?

As a pastor, I have heard countless people say, "What shocked me was who called me." "I got a letter" (or "I got a telephone call," or "Somebody spoke to me"). "Somebody at work, even though we never talked, heard what I was going through and met me at the watercooler" (or sent a note, card, flowers, or cookies).

What were these people doing? They were being an expression of the presence of a comforting God. Where is God in the worst of hurts? He is finding persons whose hearts and minds and hands He, the eternal caring God, can use to touch your painful heart.

Where is God? Wherever He is, He has not forgotten His promise: "Fear not, for I have redeemed you; I have called you by your name. You are Mine. When you pass through the waters, I will be with you. And through the rivers, they shall not overflow you" (Isa. 43:1–2).

—◈—

God Loves Me!

Thank you, Lord, for this holy sentence,
this good news, this happy report,
this exciting thought, this graceful truth,
this fantastic lesson. God loves me!
Even when I'm at my worst—God loves me.
Even when my faith is dim—God loves me anyway!
It's incomprehensible and fantastic!
Thank you, Father.
Amen.

Not Too Small for God's Love

When my daughter Carol had her leg amputated and had to be in the hospital for seven painful months, she used to say that she made it through the lonely and painful days because of the cleaning girl. The cleaning girl? Yes, a little Vietnamese girl whose family had escaped Vietnam and come to America. She could speak little English. No one had wanted to hire her because she was unqualified—except to do a job nobody wanted: emptying the wastebaskets in a hospital. . . . Every time she entered Carol's room she stopped just a minute and smiled. Then she went to the wastebasket, picked it up, and smiled again at the thirteen-year-old amputee before walking out. Day after day that loving smile gave Carol the strength to stay alive and not give up. And we don't even know the girl's name. . . .

Corrie ten Boom was a Dutch woman who was sent by Hitler to a death camp to live and die with the Jews. How she escaped was a miracle of God. I knew her well. . . . Corrie often came to visit Carol in the hospital after the accident—sometimes daily, before she herself became ill. "You must fight on!" she would say in her thick Dutch accent. "You *can!* Yes, you *can!*" She became Carol's warrior. She was as essential to Carol's recovery as were all the medical experts and the little Vietnamese cleaning girl. Each time Corrie came, she gave Carol her blessing: "Remember, no person is too small for God's love, and no problem is too big for God's power."

— ◇ —

A Plan for Your Life

I have no doubt that God has a plan for every life and He has a plan for you.

> I have a plan for your life; it is a plan for your good and not evil; it is a plan to give you a future and a hope. (Jer. 29:11)

You didn't ask to be born—you weren't your own idea. No human being ever had the chance to decide whether to be born or not. You were God's idea. Therefore it makes sense to go back to the God who conceived of your conception as a person. Ask Him, "Lord, what was your plan for me? What do you want me to do with my life?"

It's amazing how many people fail because they ignore the inventor and dream up their own ideas: What would I like to do? What would be most profitable? Then they make decisions and start off expecting everybody else to support them!

We have all read stories of explorers who took cameras and recording equipment into primitive areas only to have them destroyed by the natives. Threatened by the unfamiliar equipment, these natives became frightened. They didn't understand the purpose of the invention or of the inventor.

God created you and allowed you to be born because he wants to use you where you are. He is the inventor, and He has a specific purpose for each of His inventions—for you and me. He wants to do something beautiful with your life.

—◇—

The Person God Sees

The beggar sat across the street from an artist's studio. From his window the portrait painter sketched the face of the defeated, despairing soul—with one important change. Into the dull eyes he put the flashing glint of an inspired dreamer. He stretched the skin on the man's face to give him a look of iron will and fierce determination. When the painting was finished, he called the poor man in to see it. The beggar did not recognize himself. "Who is it?" he asked as the artist smiled quietly. Then, suspecting that he saw something of himself in this portrait, he hesitantly questioned, "Is it me? *Can* it be me?" "That's how I see you," replied the artist. Straightening his shoulders, the beggar responded, "If that's the man you see—that's the man I'll be."

God looks at you and sees a beautiful person waiting to be born! If you could see in a vision the man God meant you to be, never again could you be quiet. You'd rise up and try and succeed.

—◇—

I Am God's Idea

"Why don't you tell people what sinners they are?" I'm often asked.

The answer is obvious. People have no trouble believing they're sinners. That's easy. The most difficult task is to help people believe how beautiful they can become if they will allow the love of Christ to fill their lives! Constant positive reinforcement is an unending need. People need to be told daily, "I am God's idea—so I must be okay."

Remember: Goethe said, "Treat people as if they were what they ought to be and you help them to become what they are capable of being."

—◆—

God's Better Idea

Paint a mental picture of the *new you!* You are going to change. You are changing now. You will become the person you always wanted to be. Believe this.

Now discard all old mental pictures of yourself. These negative portraits are past history. Replace them with the future dream portrait of the person you want to become.

Computer programmers have an expression called "Gigo," which stands for Garbage In–Garbage Out. Feed garbage into the computer and garbage will come out. If you are failing, the problem is "Fifo"—failure pictures have been fed into your mind so failure comes out. Now, try the "Siso" formula! Success In– Success Out! Feed success pictures into your imagination and success *will* come out!

It's happening all around you today. Disadvantaged, defected, discouraged people are learning how to change their lives, their futures, their destinies. Now it's your turn to stop failing and start succeeding. Discover the better idea God has for your life. You are God's idea and God only dreams up beautiful ideas. He's expecting great things from you. Cooperate! Believe in yourself, *now,* and draw the possibilities out of your being.

—◇—

Beauty

Thank you, Father, for filling the world with beauty.
I thank you for the beauty of life,
the beauty of love, the beauty of children,
and the beauty of old people.
I thank you for the beauty of Christ
and for the beauty of any life
when Christ is invited through the Holy Spirit.
Thank you, Father, that you have
made my life beautiful too.
Amen.

—◇—

God's Footprints

We believe in God because we see evidences of His invisible power and might and glory in the world and in the lives of people. No one can explain for certain where the world came from or how it got here although there are a variety of "theories." We are reasonably sure that once there was nothing—now there is something.

There is, in fact, a whole universe.

As a building presupposes an architect, and a painting presupposes an artist, and a poem presupposes a poet, so the universe presupposes a Grand Architect of the ages. If I saw footprints on the beach, I would conclude that someone had been there. God's footprints are clearly seen on the shores of the immeasurable universe.

If I walked into the desert and saw a pile of rocks, I would think nothing of it. If I walked in the desert and saw a long ridge of rocks, I would think nothing of it. If I walked in the desert and saw a rock here and another there, I would think nothing of it. But if, in the middle of the desert, I came upon a neat arrangement of rocks lying in rows with one rock in the first row, two in the second row, three in the third row, four in the fourth row, five in the fifth row, and six rocks in the sixth row, and all of the rows arranged one above the other to form a perfect triangle—I would intelligently conclude that someone had been there. That is the way our universe has been put together.

Yes, there is so much evidence for a Master Mind in the universe that we can say that the reality and the existence of God is proven by the normal scientific methods of reasoning.

—◆—

Your Future Is Your Friend

The hand of the Almighty is never far away. No wonder you can trust the future! And when you cannot see any good, but only stark, naked, cruel, brutal tragedy in a catastrophic situation, then you can expect God to come and show mercy! As an unexpected gust of wind comes under the weary wings of a storm-drenched bird to lift the pitiful creature to higher altitudes where it can soar in new strength, so God comes with an unannounced invasion of mercy.

When God's goodness cannot be seen, His mercy can be experienced!

—◇—

Hands Above Our Own

What then is my faith? I believe with the Psalmist that there is an unseen God at the controls of the life that has been surrendered to Him. God will let nothing happen unless it is for our own good or for the good of God's kingdom, or for the good of others.

Make no mistake about it, there is another hand above your own! My son was nine years old and wanted badly to learn to drive my car. I let him sit between my legs and permitted his hands to grip the wheel and steer the car around the ten-acre church grounds. His little white-knuckled hands strangled the steering wheel but he managed to maneuver the turns, and bring the powerful automobile back to the parking space. When we came home to lunch, you should have heard him boast to his mother and older sister! "I drove the car, Mommy, all by myself! Really, I did!" Happy, but foolish child! I had my big hands only a fraction of an inch over his all the time, ready to clamp down and take over in case I sensed him losing control. And, unknown to him, all the while *my* foot was on the gas pedal. . . .

The hand of the Almighty is never far away. No wonder you can trust the future!

—◇—

It Is a Choice

Mercy is the declaration that our sins are forgiven. Mercy is the sudden glimmer of something new to live for. Mercy is the slender sliver of silver hope through the dark night. Mercy is the first faint, then growing, thought that I must, I will, pick up the pieces and start over again!

You want to argue the point? I refuse! It's a choice—not an argument. It must be a decision, not a debate! G. Studdert Kennedy said: "These clouds are lies. They cannot last. The blue sky is the truth, for God is Love. Such is my faith, and such my reasons for it, and I find them strong enough. And you? You want to argue? Well, I can't. It is a choice and I choose the Christ."

—◇—

I Am Eager!

*Lord, you've put the whole world together
and you've put me in the middle of it because
you want to say something to me and through me today.
May your beautiful peace fall gently, softly,
sweetly, and beautifully upon my mind—now.
I am ready to listen and eager to move ahead,
today, with "Possibility Thinking."
Amen.*

There will never be another now—I'll make the most of today. There will never be another me—I'll make the most of myself.

Are You an
Impossibility Thinker?

Impossibility Thinkers are people who make swift, sweeping passes over a proposed idea, scanning it with a sharp negative eye, looking only for the distasteful aspects. They look for reasons why something won't work instead of visualizing ways in which it could work. So they are inclined to say "No" to a proposal, never giving the idea a fair hearing.

Impossibility Thinkers are people who immediately, impulsively, instinctively, and impetuously react to any positive suggestion with a sweeping, unstudied, irresponsible assortment of reasons why it can't be done, or why it is a bad idea, or how someone else tried it and failed, or (and this is usually their clinching argument) how much it will cost! They are people who suffer from a perilous mental malignancy I call the impossibility complex. They are problem imaginators, failure predictors, trouble visualizers, obstacle envisioners, exaggerated-cost estimators.

Their attitude produces doubt, stimulates fear, and generates a mental climate of pessimism and fatigue. They are worry creators, optimism deflators, confidence squelchers. The end result? Positive ideas buried, dreams smashed, creativity aborted, and projects torpedoed.

—◇—

Or Are You a Possibility Thinker?

The Possibility Thinkers resemble the hummingbird that looks for and finds honey, often in the most unlikely and unthinkable places. The Possibility Thinkers perceptively probe every problem, proposal, and challenge to discover and disclose the positive opportunities pregnant in almost every human situation.

They are people—just like you—who when faced with a mountain do not quit. They keep on striving until they climb over, find a pass through, tunnel underneath—or simply stay and turn their mountain into a gold mine.

Why do they succeed? They have trained themselves to look for the positive possibilities in all areas of life. They have learned how to:

- Overcome inferiority complexes and live confidently
- Listen to new ideas and evaluate them carefully
- Opportunities: see them, size them, and seize them courageously
- Welcome challenging problems and solve them creatively
- Face personal tragedies with equanimity and, if possible, use them constructively

Great people! These faith builders, hope boosters, confidence creators, enthusiasm generators, optimism spreaders!

History calls them pacesetters, record breakers.

Thank God for these dedicated dreamers, these sanctified opportunists, these glorified gamblers, these powerful believers.

—◇—

Imagine the Unimaginable

A Possibility Thinking expert is a person who, when faced with a new concept and knowing that it has never been successfully implemented, is charged with excitement at what he sees as a great opportunity to become a pacesetting pioneer. He is stimulated by the opportunity to discover new solutions to old problems using the knowledge of new age to make a historic breakthrough. Because he is convinced that there must be a way to overcome seemingly insurmountable difficulties, his creative powers are stimulated to produce amazing results. Using advanced research techniques, he proves that some long-accepted causes for past failure were, in fact, errors of judgment made by intelligent researchers who lacked the tools, skills, or related knowledge available in this modern age. So failure is never final!

Just because some Negative Thinking expert says, "I can't imagine it!" that doesn't mean that someone, somewhere, sometime cannot and will not be able to "imagine the unimaginable" and, amazingly, accomplish it!

—◇—

Succeed as a Possibility Thinker

Stop the self-deceiving and self-defeating habit of defending your mistakes, rationalizing your sins, making excuses for your failures, and whitewashing your errors of judgment.

Look deeply into yourself and your situation and see the slumbering possibilities that wait to be awakened.

Listen to constructive criticism, sensible advice, and honest counsel that serious and sincere friends have been trying for years to communicate to you.

Protect Yourself

The positive mental attitude toward emotional well-being makes the person sensitive to the differences between negative and positive feelings. The Possibility Thinker gradually gains the ability to recognize and reject negative feelings, then intuitively and self-consciously senses and submits to the positive feelings! All forms of emotional input—relationships, books, magazines, religious teachings, lectures—affect our emotional well-being for better or worse. We begin to sense whether our thoughts and experiences are giving us joy, hope, confidence, courage, love. If these positive emotions are stimulated, we allow ourselves to remain in the groove. But if ideas, individuals, institutions, activities, or experiences tend to leave us with negative feelings (discouragement, depression, anger, guilt, shame), we take *immediate* corrective action to extract ourselves or, if this is not practical, create shields to protect ourselves from negative impact. My own shields are prayer and Bible verses.

—◇—

Begin Each Day with a Positive Seed Thought

Dress your mind when you dress your body. No discreet person would go into the world half dressed. No wise person will consider himself well dressed unless his mind is wearing a "positive idea" as a shield against the negative forces that will strike him before his workday begins. Make a hobby of collecting "shields for the spirit" that can fortify your mind as you move into the workaday world. Try these spirit shields:

Luke 1:37: "With God nothing shall be impossible."

Mark 10:27: "With men it is impossible, but not with God."

Matthew 19:26: "But with God all things are possible."

Mark 10:27: "For with God all things are possible."

Luke 18:27: "The things which are impossible with men are possible with God."

Mark 9:23: "If you can believe, all things are possible to him who believes."

Mark 14:36: "Father, all things are possible."

Matthew 17:20: "If you have faith as a grain of mustard seed you can say to this mountain move, and nothing shall be impossible."

Use Prayer Power

Prayer power really works! There is a Higher Power that can and will penetrate the depths of your being to recondition your thought processes. Ask God to help you to become a Possibility Thinker. Ask Him once, and never again. For if you have sent Him one petition you may be sure He has your message. Stop asking, but don't stop praying. Stop begging and start thanking. To continue to plead will only indicate your lack of faith in His hearing or helping power. To continue to ask will only generate or intensify your emotional misery. This will weaken you. It will not inspire you. It will not strengthen you. Pleading, negative praying only exercises and strengthens your anxieties. Someone said: "God weighs our prayers; He doesn't count them."

In the right way, in the right time, God will answer. So make your prayers affirmative, not negative. Thank Him for hearing your prayer. Thank Him for what He is doing about it. Try this prayer. Repeat it out loud. "Thank you, God, for making me a Possibility Thinker. Thank you for reminding me that all things are possible if I will dare to believe." This is power-generating, hope-building, anxiety-relieving prayer. Pray yourself up. Don't pray yourself down. Affirmative prayer really works miracles. This was the way Christ prayed: "Abba Father, all things are possible unto you." And when a human being asks God to save him from his impossibility complex, God will help. After all, God wants to see His sons and daughters walk with shoulders back, heads erect, with dignity shining in their faces.

—◇—

My Secret Place

This is the room Jesus talked about—the *ultimate power room*. He said, "And when you pray, enter into your closet, and when you have shut the door pray to your Father in secret and your Father who hears in this secret place will reward you—openly!" (Matt. 6:6).

What do you do in this secret room alone with your God who loves you?

Ask Him to help you choose what to throw away, what to keep. Some stuff is just shameful. He reaches for it, throws it where the trash will pile up; now He turns and smiles at you. "Isn't it fun getting rid of *that!*" He says exuberantly. "It didn't make you look good, really." He shuffles a few hangers.

"Now *this!*" He holds up and proudly shows you that beautiful and wonderful new dream. "This will bring the real beauty out in you!" He holds it in front of you. "Check this one. It's the real *you!*"

Suddenly decisive, you throw more of the tawdry, outdated stuff on the floor and reach for the new dream—one tailored just for you, tasteful, timely, and dignified! And you realize what a Savior God really is!

Possibility Thinkers: pray and prioritize! This is where your life will take aim and find direction. Set priorities *prayerfully*. God is inspiring you. The Eternal Spirit is enlightening you. A beautiful new possibility is coming to your head and heart as a bright new hope! It's yours to wear. Perfect for the new you!

I Believe

Those two words, "*I believe*," can make the difference between sinking and swimming. They can make the difference between surrendering or surviving. They can make the difference between life or death.

Do you pray? Have you ever talked to God? Do you wonder if He exists? Does He care? How can He still love you?

Start each day with these two words. Go someplace where you don't have to worry about feeling foolish. Then look out the window and say them, however tentatively, "I believe! I believe! I believe!"

Don't expect fireworks. They don't go off the first time. Or the second. Or the third. But keep it up. Keep affirming the fact that you believe! You believe in God! You believe in yourself! You believe in new tomorrows! You believe in second chances. You will be amazed at the doors of faith that this simple exercise will open for you.

———◇———

I Need Help

You believe that God can help you, but you've been afraid to ask Him. It feels selfish to pray for yourself.

Go ahead. Do it! Ask Him! He'll understand. He knows the longings of your heart. The Bible tells us, "Yet you do not have because you do not ask" (James 4:2). The truth is, many so-called selfish prayers are very humble prayers. Some of you will never find the power breakthrough you need until you dare to be "selfish" in your prayers, until you are able to say, "God, I need help! I can't do it alone." . . .

You have needs that must be prayed for: in your marriage, in your business, in your studies, at school, in relationships. God wants to help you. He wants to be your best friend.

The Bible makes it perfectly clear: "Ask, and it will be given to you" (Matt. 7:7). Ask! Let God help you. Many of you are never going to get your life together until you become humble enough to say, "I need help, Lord! I can't do it alone."

What Is Prayer?

The greatest power in the world today is the power of people to communicate with Almighty God.

Prayer is not a scheme whereby we can move God into our lives but rather a spiritual exercise through which we draw ourselves toward God until we are a part of His plan and His purpose.

The purpose of prayer is not to give you what you want when you want it but to make you the kind of person God wanted you to be when He put you on the planet earth.

—◇—

Aligned with God

When we are in harmony with God's universal plan and purpose then we have peace. When we are out of harmony with God and His universal plan and purpose, there will be inner frustration, tension, and conflict. Real prayer is the spiritual exercise of putting our dreams and desires in harmony with God's plan. . . .

True prayer is discovering the inner harmony of mind that results when you are thinking God's thoughts for your life. For example, you are in a boat. You approach the shore. You throw the anchor out until it digs into the sand. You take hold of the anchor rope and pull on it until your boat slides onto the sandy beach. What have you done? You have not moved the shore to the boat. You have moved the boat to the shore.

—◆—

No Whining!

Do not allow your prayer to turn into a crying jag, an anxiety-generating exercise, a worry-feeding talk.

No! You pack power into your prayer by jamming it with expectant thoughts.

"God—I know that you are planning something wonderful."

"God—I don't know how you are going to solve my problem, but I know you have something in mind and I thank you for it."

"God—you are going to use me in ways that I do not know, but I expect that you have something wonderful around the corner!"

I have traveled around the world often enough to know that many people who try to exercise prayer power are doing themselves more harm than good. I have seen people literally crawl in the dust, acting like worms, pouring out their pitiful pleadings to a vague deity. I have heard other people pray with a mourning cry, a wailing and a weeping singsong voice, with faces long, drawn, and anguish-torn. Such prayer is by no means true communion with God. It is the exercise of a neurotic and fearing personality. Health-producing, power-generating, self-love-creating prayer is prayer that is filled with a dynamic spirit of optimism.

Faint Not

Sometimes a secret sin harbored in the heart is enough to cause our soul and our spiritual life to become barren and dry, just as a grain of sand in the gas line of a car causes power to fail. If there is spiritual power lost in your life, check your secret heart carefully.

What shall we do when the shivering season strikes the soul? Jesus gave a beautiful answer in a parable. "Ye ought always to pray and faint not." Like the widow who kept appealing to the judge, refusing to take no for an answer, so we, too, must unceasingly pray to God. "I will not let Thee go, O Lord, except Thou bless me."

———◆———

New Toys

Of course, we get our needs and our wants all mixed up. We consider to be necessities what are, in reality, luxuries. There are only four absolutely basic human needs. We need water, food, and air, or our body will die. Without these things we cannot live. And our spirit needs emotional empowerment or our soul shall never enjoy spiritual life. These basic needs God will supply.

But there is no promise that He will give us what we want. Not infrequently, we do not know what we want. For example, we think we want a new car. In reality we want an escape from boredom, and the car "kick" constitutes a new interest, a new "cause," a new absorbing project. Often we really do not want the "thing" we are buying. What we really want is the joy of shopping, the venture of running around to break the cabin fever; or we buy to make an impression. And, too often, what we want is not the best for us. No wonder God in His mercy neglects so often to provide what we want.

—◇—

Thank You, God

God is good! Yes, He is! No matter what has happened, God is there for you. And as hard and as crazy as it may sound, when the walls collapse and the world tumbles in, and when it looks like everything that we've loved is lost, that's the time to say, "Thank you, God!"

I can hear you cringe as you read these words. "Oh! That's too hard to do. You don't know what I've lost! How can I possibly thank God? I don't want to thank Him. I want to argue with Him. I want Him to put things back the way they were."

Of course you want God to repair the damage that is deflating you, disappointing you, discouraging you, or defeating you. You want your job back. You want your money back. You want your loved one back. You want your health back. Believe me—that's the time when you need most to say, "Thank you, God."

Thank You! Thank You! Thank You!

When you lose a loved one, there is a way to thank God. You can thank Him for the promise of life eternal. You can thank Him for the assurance that someday you will be reunited with the one you've lost.

The worse the loss, the harder the fall, the deeper the pain— the more you need to say, "Thank you, Lord!"

Thank you, Lord! is the force that draws back the curtains, letting tomorrow's light pierce today's darkness.

Thank you, Lord! is the first slippery step back up from the ditch of depression.

Thank you, Lord! is the seed of faith planted in the dry, cracked earth.

When you least feel like doing it—say Thank you, Lord!

You don't say Thank you to God because you are crediting or blaming Him for your heartache. *No!* Nothing could be further from the truth! God is good! He is the father of love and goodness! Most of the time we make our own heartache. Why then do we say Thank you, Lord, in the midst of the raging storm?

We say Thank you, Lord, that you're still there to help us!

Thank you, Lord, that I'm not totally alone!

Thank you, Lord, for the help you will send me. Thank you, Lord. Thank you for tomorrows that are sure to come.

Thank you! Thank you! Thank you! It's a vital element of positive prayer.

—◇—

Help Others, Lord

My grandsons are active participants in intercessory prayer. Every night before they go to bed, they go through their list of people that they regularly pray for. The list gets longer and longer because they take this task seriously. No wonder! Time after time they have seen God answer their prayers of childlike faith. Right now their list includes a young boy who has a serious heart condition, complicated by a hole in his heart.

They pray for a mother who has a serious, life-threatening form of cancer. They pray for a little girl whose mother died last month. She cries herself to sleep at night. The boys are praying for Sarah and her tears. They are also praying for a little boy who has been having seizures. The doctors are still running tests. Meanwhile four little boys pray for him every night.

God hears these prayers. The grandmother of the little boy with the heart condition was touched by the fact that four little boys were praying every night for her grandson. She sent the boys thank-you notes. Then last month she called with news. The doctors said the hole in her grandson's heart was closing. There was no medical explanation for it. The boys knew right away why the hole was closing. They said, "It's because we've been praying for him!"

—◆—

I'm Listening, Lord

God wants to talk to you. Are you listening to what He has to say?

Have you taken the time recently to draw close to God alone?

Close the door. Wait for Him to speak to you. Become a feather in the wind, a leaf on the wave, a cloud in front of the breeze. God is the wind; He is the wave; He is the breeze. All you need to do is relax; let Him do all the work. He will carry you like a gentle breeze; He will guide you like a strong current. He will give you new thoughts, new insights that are the breakthroughs you needed.

In meditation, we stand before Him like a chunk of clay. We recognize that He is the master potter. We are willing to let Him do the molding. Our job is to stay put on the potter's wheel. In His good and gentle hands, He can mold our lives into something useful, something beautiful. After all, we tried to do it ourselves and made a pretty big mess of things.

God wants to talk to you. He has things to say that you need to hear. But we get so preoccupied with our list of things to do, we let our distractions blind us to His presence. His voice is drowned out by the din of the busy workaday world we whirl through. Sometimes it takes a tragedy or a disaster to get our attention. Sometimes it takes a disappointment or an injustice to pull us out of our dizzy, spellbinding schedule to turn our eyes up to Him, and to open our hearts to what He longs to tell us.

Are You Listening?

God waits every day for you and for me to stop for a moment and listen to Him. What an honor to think that the Lord of the universe has things that He wants to tell *you!* When was the last time you talked to Him? When was the last time He talked to you?

You say He's never talked to you? Well, maybe that's because you weren't listening. Or maybe it's because His voice was drowned out by traffic, by telephones ringing, by the rush of the calendar. God's voice is a still small voice. It will come as a positive idea "out of the blue"—or as a positive "feel-good feeling"—or as a pleasant memory coming to your mind—or as an unexpected visit from someone.

If you want to hear Him, you have to seek Him out in a quiet, all-alone kind of spot. Even Jesus withdrew to hear His Father's voice. Time and time again it tells in the Bible how Jesus retreated to a solitary place to pray. . . . He would often retreat to the mountains or to a boat in the middle of the sea. His prayers were simple conversation and communication with His best friend—His Father! . . .

If Jesus, God's Son, needed to withdraw to hear God's voice, don't you think that the same might be true for you?

—◇—

Do You Recognize God's Voice?

"God knows the things you have need of." How can you ask for something you don't even know you need? God knows what it is you need. Ask Him. He will tell you.

His voice may come in the form of an idea. It may come in the mail, a letter from someone who cares and gives you the courage to go on. God's voice can be heard through phone calls—from an old friend, a family member, "I was thinking about you today." You can hear God's voice when you read the Bible. Sometimes He even speaks through ministers or inspirational books.

You can hear God. He will talk to you—indeed He has talked to you—chances are you just didn't recognize His voice when He spoke. Open your eyes. You will see God at work in your life. Open your ears. You will hear God's voice. It's possible God is speaking to you *now* through these words!

—◆—

Use Me, Lord

How do you want to be remembered? All of us think about this from time to time. I would hope that after I have died, people would say of me, "He was an encourager." I want to encourage people, give them hope and courage. I want to be a blessing.

Anybody can be a blessing. You only need three things: a head, a heart, and hands. Yes, anyone can be a channel of a blessing to someone.

God needs you. He wants to use *you!* Prayer is much more than a cloistered life. Prayer is living out God's words. It is putting faith into action. It is a mind through which God is allowed to think. It is a heart through which God is allowed to love others. It is eyes that see into the hurting hearts of people—to sense their pain, their suffering, their disappointment, their discouragement, their worries, and their sin.

Prayer is more than words. It is a look, a word, a touch. . . .

Don't think that if you ask God to use you you will be sent to the jungles, drowned, beaten, taken hostage, or put on the firing line. God has other exciting adventures in store for you. Life may not be always fair—but it's never dull, when you ask God to use you! I wear a medallion when I preach. On it is this prayer: "Lord, lead me to the person you want to speak to through my life today."

And if God uses you, will life treat you with fairness always? That I cannot promise. I cannot promise that life will always be fair but I can promise you that God will have the last word—and it will be good!

A Life Filled with Love and Meaning

If you have approached God honestly and have sincerely asked Him to cleanse you of all guilt, if you have affirmed your faith in Him and have yielded yourself to His will, then you have every right to expect that He will do what is best for your life.

This does *not* mean that you can expect a bed of roses, everything you desire. It *does* mean that you can expect that your life will take on love and meaning. And if there is love and meaning to your life, you will be able to place great value on this person called "You."

The Bible makes it very clear that Christians are soldiers—not tourists in life. We are also servants of God, not houseguests.

Pack your prayers with expectancy, and you will begin to believe that you and God together can do great things. You will attempt the "impossible." You will succeed. You will know the great thrill of climbing a mountain! Expect things to happen—and you will give life all you've got. If you don't expect things to go right, you must not hold back, restrain yourself and produce failure by your own lack of joyful anticipation. Instead, think positive! Think bigger. Think longer. Think ultimate success and energy— even enthusiasm will rise within you.

Father, I turn these minutes over to you. Do something beautiful in my mind, in my heart, and in my life today. So I will look back and say: "I was caught up by an inspiring spirit of the eternal God in this moment of prayer." In the name of Christ I pray. Amen.

On God's Team

Perhaps the most effective prayer ever was uttered by Jesus Christ in the Garden of Gethsemane when He prayed, "My Father, all things are possible unto You. Let this cup pass from me. Nevertheless not my will, but Yours be done."

You achieve an enormous sense of self-worth when you realize that you are teamed up with God in doing wonderful work in this world. God has a plan for your life. He cannot do anything with you so long as you think that you are worthless, ineffective, and unworthy. God can only do great things through self-confident human beings. You build yourself up to self-confidence when you have pursued God, repented of your sins, affirmed His friendship and forgiveness. Now you are ready to yield your confident life to His service.

The real purpose of prayer is to draw you close to God so He can fulfill His will in your life. Many people fail in prayer simply because they use prayer to try to get "what they want, when they want it, the way they want it." Such prayer is doomed to failure.

◆

Never Alone

Captain Scott O'Grady, U.S.A.F., was shot down in his jet over enemy territory. He jetted free and landed in the forested area. He shared with me his thoughts as he would lay in the brush hearing the footfall of the enemy searching for him.

"I had six days of really exploring my relationship with God and praying consistently. Never before had I had six days where I did that twenty-four hours a day, without any worldly distractions. That's an amazing thing to say, even though I was in a place where I didn't have the right to live. I could feel people were praying for me. I wasn't praying alone. It wasn't a solo prayer. And it wasn't just from the United States of America. The prayers came from all over the world. Even though I was by myself, I was never alone."

Scott said that he was taught his faith as a young boy by a very positive-thinking Catholic teacher, who said the most important part of your life is your relationship with God. Scott had faith before his days in hiding [after being shot down in Bosnia in 1995], but that experience definitely fortified it. Scott was quick to tell our audience, "I've always considered my faith a very personal thing, something that I don't normally go out and express. But when I came back, the only thing I wanted to do was tell the entire world about what a beautiful experience I had and that it was God's love that got me through."

—◇—

Six Steps to Prayer

Pursue God. Begin by confession of sin, be specific, use harsh, embarrassing words that bluntly describe you as you are. "If with all your heart you truly seek him, you shall surely find him . . ." (Deut. 4:29).

Reexamine yourself. Ask yourself, "Am I sincerely honest?" Play no games! Make no pretenses! If your problem is doubt, then admit it. For instance, pray, "I thank you, God, that you love me even when my faith is dim, dark, and dreary."

Affirm positively what God is able to do within you. In your honesty, do remain affirmative. Negative praying only weakens you. Pray, "I know that you love me anyway. I know that you are waiting eagerly to forgive me for . . ."

Yield your self-will to God. "Not my will, but yours be done, O God" (Luke 22:42).

Expect positive results. Anticipate positive emotions, sense the joy, peace, and faith flowing into you. "If you have faith, all things are possible" (Matt. 17:30).

Rejoice! In thanking God, be specific, detail your thanks. For example, "Thank you, God, for eyes to see the faces of those I love, for ears to hear my favorite music, the sound of a friend's voice on the telephone in the middle of a lonely hour of life."

—◇—

God Flowing Through Us

Prayer is designed to draw us close to God; it is not designed to move God to our will. As Frank Laubach reminds us in his great book, *Channels of Spiritual Power*, prayer is not a bucket—it is a fountainhead. Prayer is designed to connect your life to God, that His loving spirit may flow through your life into the lives of others around you. When God is flowing through you to help other human beings, you will have the most enormous sense of self-worth you've ever experienced.

—◇—

Are You Really Happy?

Happiness—that deep inner strength that is made up of courage, faith, hope, and peace. Mix them together, and you have happiness!

Happiness—the courage to hang on in the face of severe adversity!

Happiness—the faith that God will have the last word, and it will be good!

Happiness—the hope that, even though you can only see the shadow, someday the clouds will clear away and the sun will shine again!

Happiness—the quiet sense of self-esteem that comes when you know you have done your best.

Happiness—the assurance that you have been merciful and kind to enemy and friend alike.

Happiness—the quiet assurance that God will be merciful and kind to you, too.

Happiness—the beautiful belief that this life, no matter how difficult it may be, is not your final destination.

Love Positively

If you want to live positively, you could start by learning to love positively. And that's what Jesus said, too. When the disciples came to Him and asked Him which of the commandments were the greatest, Jesus surprised them with a new commandment. It's often called the eleventh commandment. It summarizes all of the Ten Commandments into one positive commitment. Jesus said, "You shall love the Lord, your God, with all your heart, with all your mind, and with all your strength, and you shall love your neighbor as yourself."

Drive the negative fear, the negative anger, out of your life with positive love. It takes courage to love. It takes a brave heart that risks being broken to discover the joy of love.

"In love's service, only broken hearts will do."

—◇—

Risky Business

Here's a basic lesson in theology. When God gets you where He wants you, you won't be able to do what you have to do without risk. Naturally; that's what the word "faith" means. When God lays His dream for your life into your thinking, it will be humanly impossible. That's His way of making sure you (1) have faith, (2) will seek His help, (3) can be trusted with the grand success He plans as a surprise at the top of the peak.

Thank you, Father, for the beautiful surprises
you are planning for me today.
So often in my life, when it looked like the day
would be dismal, depressing, and dark,
an unexpected burst of golden sunshine exploded
through a black cloud sending inspiring shafts
of warm, beautiful sunshine into my life.
Father, it is happening now! I can already feel
the power of your love, through Christ my Lord.
Amen.

◈

Feathers in the Wind

I suppose everybody knows something bad somebody has done somewhere along the line. Forget it. Why tell somebody else about it? In the book of Proverbs, we read these words, "Where there is no wood, the fire goes out." Where there is no one to tell tales, the memory dies. I cannot resist underlining a well-circulated story here. Once there was a Catholic priest who made calls regularly in the home of a young widow. Somebody started passing a rumor. Some busybody began to be suspicious. Two ladies "put two and two together" and began to gossip. Suddenly the young widow died and the community was informed that she had been secretly sick with cancer. Only her priest knew about it. He came regularly to pray for her and to help her. But someone with a dirty mind had started talking. The two ladies who were responsible for it all came to the priest and said, "We are sorry, truly sorry. Why didn't you tell us, Father?" (A priest or a minister frequently cannot defend himself without violating somebody else's confidence.) The priest answered, "All right, if you're sorry, take this feather pillow, go to the top of the hill, and let the feathers fly where the wind will carry them." And they did. When they came back with their empty pillowcase they said, "Father, we have done this. Now, will you forgive us?" The priest answered, "Not until you go out and pick up every feather and put them all back in the sack and bring it back to me." They said, "But that is impossible, Father. The winds have blown the feathers to the four corners." To which he replied, "So it is with your words."

—◆—

The Broad Way . . .

Jesus Christ, the Master Teacher, wisely shared this principle two thousand years ago: "Wide is the road that leads to destruction and many are walking that dismal trail. But narrow is the way that leads to life and few there are that find it" (Matt. 7:13, 14).

What's Jesus really saying? There are two tracks we can take.

The *broad track*, which leads to final futility, folly, and failure, is the track I call *Impossibility Thinking*. Its popular appeal exploits the fears and inferiority complexes of insecure humans. "You can't do it." "You're too young [or too old]." "You don't have the money, the organization, the rich friends, the education, the talent or skill, or the impressive record in school and society to be a real success." "Face it," the negative cultural exploiters of the have-nots declare: "You don't have the color, culture, credentials, or connections to make it in today's world." They say, "Accept your fate, which is to live your insignificant life on a low-potential level." "Bury your beautiful—but impossible—dreams." "Settle for the stimulation you can buy in a bag, a bottle, a bed, or a bar!" "Go with the easy flow."

This is the broad way. You can choose to surrender leadership over your destiny to fears, to negative-thinking "friends" and family, to social and political forces that would intimidate and manipulate you until you've surrendered your personal potential, becoming only a puppet, a product, or a possession someone owns and uses for his or her own end.

◆

And the Narrow Way . . .

Then there's the *narrow way*. It's another option. It too is yours to choose. But it isn't just another variation of the broad way. It's a totally alternative decision. I call it *Possibility Thinking*. It's a competing, challenging, and truly creative option.

Yes, there are two tracks you can take. It's your choice. You're free to decide.

What a narrow way Possibility Thinking is! "I may not have the money—but I can make a little, save a little, earn more, and reach my goal anyway!"

"I may not have the training, the education, or the intelligence, but I've got something more important than a high IQ. I've got a high EQ—emotional quotient!" A high EQ is a heart that has strong faith, unquenchable hope, and passionate love. Listen to the high-EQ person: "I can get smart, or meet and hire people who are smarter than I am! I can choose any dream I want—and go for it."

Two tracks. One is narrow—that's the high-EQ route. One is broad—that's the low-EQ route. You may choose which path to take: Impossibility Thinking or Possibility Thinking!

Broad is the road that leads to failure and futility. Narrow is the way that leads to success and achievement. Attack your impossibility complex and attach yourself to Possibility Thinkers!

Creative Poise

Keep a strong possibility posture as you confront your problem with creative poise. You will use Possibility Thinking to:

- *Remind yourself* that every problem is an unfilled need.

- *Remember* that success is finding a need and filling it.

- *View* your problem as an opportunity in disguise.

- *Welcome* your problem as a guideline or challenge.

- *Look for and find someone somewhere* who can help you solve or sublimate this problem.

If you live near the ocean, watch the waves roll in. You may see a timid swimmer who, spotting a great wave rising, panics, turns, and runs, only to be overcome by the rushing mountain of water and sent tumbling and sputtering in the surf. Now watch the surfer. He looks for and sees the savage wave swelling. He welcomes the wave with the spirit of Caleb, "Give me a mountain!" He is poised with a surfboard in his hands. As the rising, racing wave reaches full crest this Possibility Thinker mounts the liquid mountain and is lifted high and carried far!

Face your problems with creative poise and you will never be defeated.

Stick It Out

Tough times never last, but tough people do. Tough people stick it out. They have learned to choose the most positive reaction in managing problems. And that's the real key: "managing problems." For in spite of all of our Possibility Thinking, there are after all some problems that defy solutions.

If your leg is amputated, you can't grow it back. You can manage this problem, however, by considering all the possible ways in which a prosthesis can be developed, improved, and refined. You can manage it by determining to walk better, more smoothly, more quickly than anybody else could imagine. In the process you will become an inspiration to everyone whose life touches yours.

Possibility Thinking—I do not claim that it can solve every problem. But I have no doubt that the vast majority of problems can be solved if we only believe. "With you this is impossible; but with God all things are possible" (Matt. 19:26).

—◇—

The Power of Possible

When uttered aloud, the word "impossible" is devastating in its effect on the subconscious. Thinking stops. Progress halts. Doors slam shut. Research comes to a screeching halt. Further experimentation is torpedoed. Projects are abandoned. Dreams are discarded. The brightest and the best of the creative brain cells nose-dive, clam up, hide out, cool down, and turn off in some dark but safe subterranean corner of the mind. By means of this defensive maneuver, the brain shelters itself against the painful sting of insulting disappointments, brutal, embarrassing rejections, and dashed hopes.

Now let someone utter the magic words, "It might be possible! I don't know *how*, or *when*, but it *might* be possible!" Those stirring words, with the siren appeal of a marshaling trumpet, penetrate into the subconscious tributaries of the mind, challenging and calling those proud powers to turn on and turn out! Buried dreams are resurrected. Sparks of fresh enthusiasm flicker, then burst into new flame. Tabled motions are brought back to the floor. Dusty files are reopened. Lights go on again in the long-darkened laboratories. Telephones start ringing. Computers light up. New budgets are revised and adopted. "Help Wanted" signs are hung out. Factories are retooled and reopened. New products appear. New markets open. The recession ends. A great new era of adventure, experimentation, expansion, and prosperity is born.

---◆---

A Most Dangerous Word

Impossible? . . . It's not in my dictionary! That's because "impossible" is a dangerous word!

Impossible? The word has the destructive power of an emotional thermonuclear bomb!

Impossible? That word is a knife thrust at the heart of creativity!

Impossible? That word is a roadblock to progress!

Let's unmask the word. We need to label these impossibilities correctly. They may be more honestly called:

- Prejudices!
- Challenges!
- Problems to be solved!
- Blind spots!
- Fatigue!

- Ignorance!
- Fear!
- Excuses!
- Ego problems!
- Laziness!

Call these "impossibilities" by their right name: *fears* that are taking over leadership in our thought processes. They are the stubborn mental fences built by ignorance, apathy, or intolerance. Strip the mask from those "It's impossible's" and what do you find? A partial perception which produces illusion, which in turn produces confusion.

—◇—

Feed Yourself Good Things

If you want something worthwhile to come out of your mind, you have to put something worthwhile into it. Cultivate the discriminatory art. Does this television program, this literature, this conversation, inspire me? Or does it depress me? Does it help me want to be a better person, or is it neutral and unstimulating? Does it evoke the positive emotions of love, faith, hope, and joy, or the negative emotions of hate, disbelief, fear, and misery? Am I feeding my mind a diet that will calm, challenge, uplift, or inject determination to go out and win?

Stop listening to those Impossibility Thinkers who tell you how wrong you are—how impossible your idea is.

As much as possible discipline yourself to an exposure to positivism. Go to the library and find books that will teach you more on the art of becoming a Possibility Thinker. There are many.

Weekly Refreshment

A friend of mine who has had problems with dandruff said, "Every Saturday night, without fail, I have to add to my usual shampoo a special dandruff-fighting solution. This keeps my problem under control for one week."

Well, once a week we should give ourselves a spiritual- and mental-dandruff-removing treatment. Skip a week and you will feel the difference. Skip two weeks and others will tell the difference.

God knew what He was doing when He ordered the ancient Jews to reserve one day in seven for rest and worship. The rising tide of emotional problems in our country has escalated with the simultaneous rise in a breakdown of the practice of setting one day aside for quietness, rest, and the refreshment of the spirit. Find a place of religious worship that specializes in positive inspiration, and attend weekly. The human being's inspiration tank needs to be refilled every seven days. That's the way God designed us. Often it's when you don't feel like going to church that you need it most. Your lack of desire for worship is a sure sign that you need inspiration, just as the unenthusiastic sputtering of a slowing car is a certain sign that it is running out of gas.

—◇—

The Power of Positive Prayer

Pack praise and thanksgiving into your prayer and you will put power into it. Thank God for what He has done and for what He is planning to do. Thank God for the possibilities that you have to be useful and needed in life. Thank God for giving you complete freedom from guilt. Count your many blessings. Name them one by one, and you will be surprised at what the Lord has done. Jam your prayers with statements of positive thinking. Fatigue, depression, despair, defeat will depart from you. Hopefulness, cheerfulness, buoyancy will take over your spirits. Thank God for your problems. They are opportunities in disguise. Thank God you don't know what the future holds for you—it means He's still working on it! Thank God for all of your assets. Think of what you have. Eyes to see? Ears to hear? Fingers? Hands that can write? Thank God that Christ is living in you; that He is loving people through you.

—◆—

A Prayer for Change

O God, when a life has been so richly blessed as mine has been, it is not right for me not to be laughing! I confess that I am responsible for my moods. I have no right to selfishly indulge in negative feelings of self-pity.

It's time for me to change my mental dial, Lord. You are helping me. This will be the moment when the sun breaks through the parted clouds, and the springtime returns after winter.

Thank you, Lord! The dreary, depressing, disconsolate mood disappears like the morning mist in the glowing sunshine of your love.

And joy moves in!

And hope begins to build up within me!

And a beautiful feeling of love starts to surround me!

Thank you, God, for the great things you are doing within me now in this moment of prayer. Amen.

—◇—

Practice Purity of Heart

If there is a negative emotion within you that is blocking you in your relationship with God, *clean up!* "Blessed are the pure in heart, for they shall see God." Here are some exercises to help you:

1. Think of some hidden hurt in your past and pray a forgiving prayer for the person who was the cause of your hurt. C. S. Lewis said it: "We all agree that forgiveness is a beautiful idea until we have to practice it!"

2. Think of someone of whom you are jealous, and pray for that person's continued prosperity.

3. Think of someone you've hurt, cheated, insulted, slighted, snubbed, or criticized. Call him or her. Invite this person to have dinner or lunch with you. Confess to him or her your un-Christian attitude, and ask for forgiveness.

4. Think of some neglected cause, project, or person. Surprise yourself with a streak of generosity! Really give a lot—of yourself and of your substance.

5. Pray a totally honest prayer to Christ. You doubt God? Tell Him so. He'll still love you, even if you don't believe in Him! (God specializes in loving sinners!)

———◇———

Finding Purity

"Blessed are the pure in heart." It is always wise to give up anything that you think might be blocking you from a clear relationship with God. . . .

The times I felt closest to God were the times when I gave up something I desired very much. My experience proves the words of our Lord, who said, "If any man would come after me, let him deny himself and take up the cross and follow me." . . .

Years ago, I smoked. You must understand that there were no cultural biases against smoking in the community where I grew up. In my childhood church, all good Dutch preachers smoked cigars or pipes. However, I became convinced that, for me, smoking was not right, and I gave the habit up. It was difficult, but once I had quit, I felt great.

You see, fasting and tithing and giving up smoking were all part of the principle of doing something difficult with God's help and making it a success. It was an adventure of walking by faith which gave God a chance to prove Himself to me. And He did!

Now, please understand that I am not saying you have to quit smoking or lose weight before you can "see God." But I am suggesting that becoming "pure in heart" may mean you have to give up something you like very much. It may be money. It may be smoking. It may be overeating. It may be alcohol or other habit-forming drugs. It may be extramarital sex. I do not know what it is that is blocking you from a close relationship with God. I don't *want* to know what it is; that is between you and Him. But make it a spiritual adventure and you will have an experience with God.

For They Are Comforted . . .

"Why do bad things happen to good people?" This is the wrong question, because it's the one question God never answers.

The Old Testament prophets lamented in times of trouble, *"Why, O Lord?"* Always He remained silent to that question. Even when Jesus Himself cried out from the cross, "My God, my God, *why?"* God didn't answer.

God never answers the *why,* because the person who asks "why" doesn't really want an explanation; he wants an argument! God refuses to be drawn into an argument. If God answered one "why," we would come with another. There would be no end to it.

If the wrong question is *"Why do bad things happen to good people?"* then what is the right question? It is *"What happens to good people when bad things happen to them?"*

Jesus answered that question in the Beatitudes. In the second Beatitude, . . . the reality of tough situations is confronted head-on. Jesus says, in essence, "When bad things happen to good people, they are blessed, for they are comforted."

Christianity isn't a Pollyanna religion. It doesn't claim that bad things won't happen to us. We are never told in the Old or New Testament that if we live a good life we'll never have any sickness or tragedy. However, we are promised in Isaiah 43: "Fear not, for I have redeemed you; I have called you by name, you are mine. When you pass through the waters . . . they shall not overwhelm you; when you walk through fire you shall not be burned, and the flame shall not consume you. For I am the Lord your God" (vv. 1–3).

◈

Don't Blame God

Consider for a minute the dilemmas that God faced at the dawn of creation. When God created humankind, His objective was to make a material form of life which would be a reflection of His own nonmaterial Self. Thus, He chose to make man "after His image," a decision-making creature, capable of discernment, judgment, evaluation, choice, and decision.

When God created such a person, He realized fully that this creature would have the power to decide against God. But let's look at the alternative. If He had designed a man who could never make a wrong decision, this creature would never be able to make a personal decision of his own. He would be nothing but a perfect, sinless, guiltless, error-free . . . person? No! Machine? Yes! Computer? Yes! Human being . . . *never!* God decided to take the greatest gamble of the ages—to make an opinion-forming, idea-collecting, decision-making creature. What He created was a potential sinner, but a potentially loving person as well.

Don't blame God for permitting sin. Thank God that He has never, in spite of our sins, taken our freedom from us, and with it our capability of becoming sincere, loving persons.

Don't blame God for the suffering in this world! Blame human beings for personally choosing the path leading to heartache and sorrow. Blame human beings for rejecting the divine truth when it was shown to them. Blame human beings for refusing God's salvation, even when offered in the name of Jesus! You have but to look at the cross and know that no human being can ever blame God for not going to the limit to save us.

—◇—

Hold On to the Eternal

You can go out with joy if you will guard the rest of your values against the possibility of suffering damage from what's happening. When you move from one passage in life to another, when you leave one era of your life completely behind you never to return, do not leave behind the ideals, the values, the morals, and the ethics.

Maybe you're single, through decision, death, or divorce. This does not now give you the liberty to forsake your morals and ideals. Maybe you've been passed by for a promotion or perhaps you're out looking for a job. This doesn't free you from the ethical restraints by which you've lived.

There must be abiding, eternal, spiritual values around which your life will continue to move. These are the spokes on the wheel of spiritual values from which you should never depart.

Picking Up Behind Us

And often God is good in ways beyond our knowledge. God does so much for us that we never know about! His goodness *"follows"* us. That means that we never see a great deal of good that God does as He follows in our track. It is like a mother or a father who picks up after the children long after they are asleep in their beds. A son plants his little flower in the garden and does a poor job of it. After he has gone to the street to play, his father finishes the job, and corrects his son's mistakes. But the son never knows it, and the flower grows and blooms. Weeks later the son calls his friends in and brags about his expert gardening. He does not realize that the plant would have withered and died if his father had not replanted it in soft, moist soil.

God is always picking up after us. Recently a lady came into my office burdened with negatively emotional regrets. She was miserable worrying about mistakes she had made in her lifetime. "Did you ever ask God to forgive you?" I asked. "Oh, yes," she answered. "Then forget about it," I told her, continuing, "I will not even pray about it this morning. I will not even ask God to forgive you your mistakes. If you could go back and find the people you have offended you would discover that they have forgotten all about it. They would say that time has healed the wounds. The truth is that God has been following after you and has corrected your mistakes."

——◇——

No Strings Attached

Christianity is a religion based on mercy. It is rooted in forgiveness. Of all the religions in the world, Christianity is the only belief system that accepts grace as its source of salvation. Every other religion is based on good works—work hard enough or be good enough and you will earn your salvation, your heaven, your Nirvana.

Christianity alone says, "You can't do it. No one is perfect. We all make mistakes. We all suffer from guilt and shame. We are all victims. But Jesus has died on the cross with these final words: 'Father, forgive them, for they do not know what they do' (Luke 23:34). He has risen again. He has paid for my sins. He has paid for yours. The gift of salvation is *free*—no strings attached."

◈

Start Over!

Are you suffering from a hurt that is self-inflicted? Do you hate yourself for what you have done? Maybe you are cheating on your wife, or your wife is cheating on you. Maybe you are stealing from your employer, or you are dishonest and you hate like Hades the person you see in the mirror.

Oh, God, you say, *if there were just some way to tear out the black page and start over again!*

There is! You can disperse your hurt!

Say, *Jesus Christ, take me, cleanse me, forgive me. God, if you forgive me, I will be able to live with myself.*

Start over fresh and clean!

---◇---

True Repentance

Negative repentance ... will drain you of your enthusiasm. It says, "I am nothing. I am worthless. I am bad." Righteousness will not evolve from such negativity.

Positive repentance, on the other hand, says:

- "I'm sorry I didn't believe in God's dreams. From now on I will."

- "I'm sorry for not loving myself as much as the Lord did when He died on the cross for me. From now on I'll remember God loves me—and I will try to love me, too."

- "I'm sorry I was so selfish that I surrendered to the fear of failure; I didn't want people to laugh at me. From now on I'll attempt to do something great for God."

- "I now commit myself to righteousness! I will do the right thing. I will respond to the dreams God gives me—even if they seem impossible."

A Broken and Contrite Heart

Oh, the power of those restorative words, "I'm sorry!" They heal relationships—between ourselves and our friends and loved ones, and between ourselves and our Lord.

The Psalmist wrote, "A broken and contrite heart, O God, thou wilt not despise" (Ps. 51:17).

He wrote for many. Throughout the Scriptures we see them— the broken and contrite: the penitent thief; the prodigal son; David, the adulterer; Saul of Tarsus, a murderer of Christians; Mary Magdalene, the prostitute.

These scalawags—what do they all have in common? They all belong to God's Hall of Fame. In the corridors of heaven they all have positions of honor.

How did they acquire such noble recognition? All of them reached a point in their personal shortcomings, sin, and shame when they cried out, "O God, be merciful to me, a sinner!"

Yes, if your life is in a mess, stress can lead to real success—for after all, real success is being admitted to the kingdom of heaven.

You and I need this humble attitude, to be poor in spirit, in our spiritual lives. You and I need it in our prayer lives. . . .

"Blessed are the poor in spirit, for theirs is the kingdom of heaven." If you have a need, God has an answer. He specializes in matching up answers to problems, healings to hurts, and solutions to perplexing situations.

Blocking the Flow of God

I love a story I once heard about Leonardo da Vinci. According to the legend, some lads were visiting the famous artist. One of them knocked over a stack of canvases. This upset the artist because he was working very quietly and sensitively. He became angry, threw his brush, and hurled some harsh words to the hapless little fellow, who ran crying from the studio.

The artist was now alone again, and he tried to continue his work. He was trying to paint the face of Jesus, but he couldn't do it. His creativity had stopped.

Leonardo da Vinci put down his brush. He went out and walked the streets and the alleys until he found the little boy. He said, "I'm sorry, son; I shouldn't have spoken so harshly. Forgive me, even as Christ forgives. I have done something worse than you. You only knocked over the canvases. But I, by my anger, blocked the flow of God into my life. Will you come back with me?"

He took the boy back into the studio with him. They smiled as the face of Jesus came quite naturally from the master's brush. That face has been an inspiration to millions ever since.

For Renewal

*Almighty God, it is a beautiful way to live
to know that you are there with a plan for my life, and
through prayer I can draw my life into harmony with your plan.
I know, God, that your plan for my life calls for me
to follow Christ. Jesus Christ, I give my life to you.
I've never done it before. That has been my problem.
That has been my hang-up.
O God, I give my life to you now.
Take my life, Jesus Christ, and make it yours.
Forgive my sins. Fill me with your love.
You are doing it now and I thank you.
Amen.*

Confession Is Good for the Soul

Confess your sins or shortcomings to God. Be honest about it. Say, "God, you know that I have often claimed to believe in you when I really haven't. But I'm thrilled to know that you love me even though I have my doubts about you at times. I'm glad to know that you want to be my friend, even though you know that I'm not a perfect person. You know I have a tough time loving myself because I"—(and here openly speak out your fears, worries, guilt).

As has often been noted, confession is good for the soul. You will never eliminate the guilt which keeps you from loving yourself until you get it into the open. Until you confess to your guilt, you will continue to rationalize, make excuses and fail to face up to your own sins and shortcomings. They do exist, be sure of that! Reexamination of yourself will lead to feelings of guilt; guilt will lead to confession; confession will lead to genuine repentance. This is the road to being born again, into a new self.

God, I have not been living according to your will.
I have only been doing what I want to do.
I have been sinning. I have been disobedient.
I give you now the areas of my life that need to be cleansed.
Jesus Christ, save me.
Amen.

—◆—

First, Accept God's Mercy

Throughout the Scriptures God promises that He will be merciful to us:

- "His *mercy* is on those who fear [trust] him" (Luke 1:50).

- "God, who is rich in *mercy*, out of the great love with which he loved us . . . made us alive together with Christ" (Eph. 2:46).

- "He saved us, not because of deeds done by us in righteousness, but in virtue of his own *mercy*" (Titus 3:5).

The promise is there! It is for *you!* What wonderful news! What wonderful assurance! No matter where our road will lead, no matter what pain may hit, no matter what we do, God will be there with His mercy to forgive us, to hold us up, and carry us through the tough times. But this is only half of the Beatitude: ". . . for they shall obtain mercy." The other half is, "Blessed are the merciful. . . ."

The question is: Which comes first? Do we need to be merciful before God will be merciful to us? Or does God need to be merciful to us before we can be merciful to others? What did Jesus mean when He said, "Blessed are the merciful, for they shall obtain mercy"?

I believe Jesus meant God will be merciful to us, then we will be merciful to others. Mercy will then come from a variety of sources.

———◇———

Accept God's Forgiveness

Forgiveness is where we run face-to-face with God's goodness. We live with many things, but we cannot live in guilt and shame; we cannot live without experiencing God's forgiveness.

The Bible says, "As far as the east is from the west, so far has He removed our transgressions from us" (Ps. 103:12).

Look at the globe. Our understanding of geography tells us that if we run our finger along the equator we will keep going east, east, east. We never hit west, unless we suddenly change directions, pivot our finger and go the opposite direction. But take your finger and go from the North Pole to the South Pole. From north to south there is an equator—a definite beginning and ending place, but going east to west is like an unbroken circle; there is no beginning and no ending. . . .

The Creator tells us that He has removed our transgressions from east to west, not from north to south. That implies that He has removed our sins forever from us. What a comfort that is. What a relief!

God has forgiven. That is a fact of life too. The gift is extended. God stands before you with a lovely gift. It is large, beautifully wrapped. He smiles at you and says, "For you. From me, with love."

—◇—

How to Experience Forgiveness

- *Reveal yourself* to a wonderful person who is deeply committed to all that is beautiful in life.

- *Risk rejection* as you openly confess your guilt to him.

- *Experience acceptance.* Shocked, you will discover that instead of shaming you, he accepts you.

- *Encounter real love in action.* Now you will be experiencing real love—a rare experience. Most love that we experience is a calculating, counterfeit affection. . . . Real love is unconditional, uncalculating, nonselective, and nonjudgmental.

- *Start loving people this way.* Experiencing unconditional love will make you feel so great that you'll start loving people in the same unconditional, nonjudgmental way.

- *Expect people to accept you.* We tend to expect people to treat us the same way we treat others. Criticize and condemn people and you'll be suspicious—you will then expect people to criticize and condemn you too. The reverse is equally true. If you love everyone with an unconditional love, you'll believe they love you in the same way. Your guilt will suddenly disappear! No longer are you fearful of exposure, condemnation, and judgment!

Try to find that wonderful person from whom you can experience and learn nonjudgmental love.

———◇———

The Work of Restoration

You're like a piece of furniture covered with layer upon layer of ancient paint. Peel, scrape, and wash off the layers of camouflaging enamel and discover the rare woods underneath! From childhood on you have been covering your real self under layers upon layers of self-criticism. You can peel off those layers of self-condemnation and expose a great heart deep down inside! . . .

While the old paint may be stripped off, there still remain the stains of self-condemnation, regret, and remorse which must be eliminated. You may have conquered your guilt to the point where you realize that God has forgiven you, but you probably still are not forgiving yourself. You still recall and ponder some of the mistakes of your past.

Although it may be difficult to keep self-despising memories from coming to mind, you don't have to give them a hearty welcome! Don't invite them in for a visit! Slam the door in their faces. God has forgiven you. Forgive yourself. When you bury the hatchet, bury it deep. Don't leave the handle above the ground. Simply affirm, "Christ lives within me—so I am a wonderful person. Christ has forgiven me. I have forgiven myself." Keep repeating these affirmations, and find yourself forgiving yourself.

Now stand up straight. Face the sun. Smile and once more repeat the affirmations aloud. It may be necessary to find a lonely spot where you can shout these affirmations as loud as possible. Actually shout them out! For the subconscious mind is sometimes only reached through enormous vocal volume.

—◆—

Affirm God's Love

Accept God's love and forgiveness. Don't keep on confessing your sins. Don't continue to tell God what a miserable person you are. To continue to do so will only feed the negative self-image you have of yourself. Now is the time to stop repenting and start affirming: "God loves me. God loves me even though I am not perfect. God loves me even though I do not have the faith that I ought to have. This must mean I am a wonderful person."

From this point on, abolish all negative statements from your prayer activity. You can pray yourself into a great and wonderful self-concept, or you can pray yourself into believing you are still a miserable, inadequate, inferior, ineffective person. The Bible says, "God is faithful and just. If we confess our sins God is faithful to forgive us of all of our iniquities." This means that if you have truly exercised the catharsis of confession you are forgiven and clean. Affirm *out loud:* "I am God's friend. God loves me. If God has chosen me for His friend I must be a marvelous person."

Probably the hardest assignment in this book will be regularly, vocally, positively to repeat these self-confidence-generating affirmations.

"I can do all things through Christ who strengthens me." I have powers within me that I have not uncovered. I have great potentialities. I can accomplish impossible feats because God and I are working together.

—◇—

Who Is Able to
Overcome the Hurt?

Is it possible to forgive?

Yes. Yes. Yes. It's not easy. Forgiving is probably the hardest task we face in our lifetimes. Yet the alternative is unthinkable—life filled with bitterness, hate, anger. There is nothing sweet about revenge. It may help to remind yourself that only to the victim of unfairness, injustice, or abuse is given the glorious opportunity to offer pardon and forgiveness!

The foundation of my faith—of Christianity—is forgiveness. The taproot of my belief system is mercy. We Christians believe in wiping the slate clean. We believe in new chances. Repairing the breaches. We follow a Leader who lived and died for forgiveness.

When Peter asked Jesus, "Lord, how often shall my brother sin against me, and I forgive him? . . . seven times?" Jesus said to him, "I do not say to you, up to seven times, but up to seventy times seven" (Matt. 18:21–22).

Yet forgiveness has been difficult for me. I am human and like you I have had my share of hurts, potshots, lies, betrayals hurled in my direction. I would be lying if I said all that didn't hurt. I have had to forgive and it has not always been easy. As a pastor I have learned as much in this area as I have taught. My people have taught me a lot about forgiveness.

—◇—

The Face of Mercy

There are some apparent human tragedies that defy the imagination; we cannot see the goodness of God in these catastrophes. . . . What can we say when there is no evidence of God's goodness? What can we say when with all our positive thinking we cannot possibly see anything good in what has happened? *Then God will show His other face. And this is the face of mercy.* Nothing will ever happen to you unless it is good, good for you, good for God, good for someone else. If anything ever befalls you that does not appear to be good for you, for God, or for anyone else, but is only the result of sin or of some terrible blunder, then you can expect a redeeming sympathy and the kiss of God's tender mercy. And if God will come to comfort, you and I can take anything! "Surely goodness and mercy shall follow me all the days of my life" (Ps. 23).

———◇———

Pardon Those Who
Have Hurt You

One of the most difficult things to do is to forgive someone who has hurt you. Again, we take a lesson from Jesus in dealing positively with our persecution.

When he was on the cross, stripped of his dignity, Jesus cried out, "Father, forgive them, for they know not what they do!"

Sometimes it is humanly impossible to forgive. When that happens, we need to call upon divine intervention. We ask God to forgive those who hurt us and to work on our hearts so that we can eventually see our hurt from their perspective.

Frequently, more often than not, people who hurt others through their words or their actions are unaware that they've injured anybody. They "know not what they do."

Other times, they are incapable of being held accountable for their actions. "They know not what they do" in terms of being so mixed up, so troubled, so spiteful, or so insecure that they act purely out of gut instinct. They are incapable of thinking about others' feelings or others' lives.

Have you been hurt? Are you still carrying that pain within? Is it impossible to forgive and forget? Then start by saying the prayer Christ prayed: "Father, forgive them, for they know not what they do."

—◇—

Shocking Grace

The story is told by historian Clarence McCartney of a Baptist pastor who had a terrible problem with a difficult member of his congregation during the time of the American Revolution. One day that difficult young man joined the army of General George Washington. He betrayed the army and was sentenced to be executed. The Baptist pastor walked seventy miles, hoping to pray with the young man before his execution.

The pastor arrived at the army camp. He spoke to General Washington and appealed for forgiveness and pardon. General Washington heard him out, then said, "I am very sorry, but I can do nothing for your friend."

The pastor said, "My friend? My friend? He's not my friend! He's my enemy."

When General George Washington heard that, he said, "If you would walk that far through the snow and the ice to save an enemy, then I will pardon him."

This gift called pardon, forgiveness, grace, is shocking! Incredible! You will not find such grace of human spirit portrayed anywhere as vividly as in the history of Christianity.

Before you dismiss Jesus Christ you have to decide upon those whose lives He has changed. Of course there are the hypocrites—every belief system has them. But before you condemn the faith because of its sins remember this: Christianity has the distinction of being the one religion that more than any other belief system spends billions of dollars to try to talk Gentiles, sinners, and bad people into joining its ranks!

To Change Your World, Change Yourself

"Blessed are the merciful, for they shall obtain mercy." Service is its own reward. A prescription for joyful living is: "Be good, be kind, be unselfish. Do unto others as you would have them do unto you."

If you want positive things to happen, you must be positive. If you want to be friendly with people and if you want people to be friendly toward you, be friendly to them. If you are surrounded by undesirable people, change them into good people.

How do you change them into good people? Bring the best out of them! How do you bring the best out of them? Call attention to the best that is within them! Until they begin to believe they are beautiful people, they will not treat you beautifully. . . .

If you want to change your world, change yourself. How do you change yourself? How do you become this kind of positive-thinking person? I know only one way. Education does not do it. Legislation does not do it. However, there is a living God—and a living Christ—who does. Christ can come into hearts that are filled with fear, anger, bitterness, and hurt, and He can liberate them with His mercy. It can happen to you. It happens when you meet Jesus Christ and ask Him to take over your life.

◆

Blessed Are the Merciful,
for They Shall Obtain Mercy

Learn to live by this refreshing happy attitude: "It's not what happens to me that matters most; it's how I react to what happens to me."

Be sure of this: if you have the attitude that you should forever be spared from all pain, hurt, and grief, you can be positive that someday you will be jolted with a depressing disillusionment. Sorrow, rejection, bereavement hit all of us at some point in our lives. To expect that somehow we are privileged persons and should be immune from hurt and hardship is unrealistic.

Some even feel, "Because I am a Christian, I should experience no pain and suffering. Because I'm a God-fearing person and a good person, I should experience no rejection or ridicule." If this is our attitude, we will react to adversity with self-pity. "It's not fair!" will be our immediate negative reaction. But the quicker we learn that life is *not* always fair, the sooner we can achieve emotional maturity.

—◇—

Unexpected Showers
of Tenderness

At the darkest time in life, and at the weariest moment of our existence, when it appears that God has forsaken or forgotten us, when we cannot comprehend or see evidence of the goodness of God, He will come and bestow mercy and tenderness. If, in your time of tragedy, you will cling with a childlike faith to God He will visit you with a tender kiss of mercy.

I remember a day when I endured a weird assortment of irritations, conflicts, and tensions. I finally arrived home at five-thirty, went to my bedroom, tried in vain to relax, and prayed without any apparent relief. Then suddenly God answered my prayer in a most remarkable way. My bedroom door opened. Slowly, cautiously, my little girl peeked through the opening of the doorway. Her big brown eyes appeared through the slot in the door and, judging that it was safe, she suddenly threw the door wide open, ran to the edge of the bed, and the next thing I knew her soft silky hair was flowing over my eyelids and caressing my lips. Her soft cheek was on mine. She kissed and hugged me, then drew swiftly back as if she was expecting me to say, "What do you want?" And she said, "I just wanted to kiss you, because I love you, Daddy." And abruptly she whirled out, skipping and running, and the door closed behind her. She was gone, but I found myself relaxed. I drew strength from this unexpected invasion of affection. So God comes at the trying time with an unexpected shower of tenderness.

Consider Christ

Are you hungry? Thirsty? Nothing satisfies? It is your instinctive craving for God! Allow me a final plea. I am positive I have the answer for you! Give me a chance to prove it. There are three philosophies of life. (1) "What's mine is mine; I'm going to keep it." This is selfishness. It will make you miserable. (2) "What's yours is mine; I'm going to get it." This is greed. It will drain you of all joy. (3) "What's mine is yours too; I want to share it." This is Christianity! It makes you feel good when you are good to those around you, and it makes you feel God-like when you are generous to those who don't expect it and don't deserve it! God comes into your life when you give yourself away to Him and humanity in loving service.

Want evidence? Consider Christ! What a full life He lived! Full of faith, joy, purpose, peace, and power. Why? Eternity was His friend! That's one reason. And He lived to love and serve. He was always busy giving Himself away. While His blood was dripping, someone said: "He saved others—Himself He cannot save." Quite true! If you want to fill your life you have to pour it out! *Involvement is the only indulgence that really satisfies!*

—◇—

Money Matters

"Getting" always comes to the "giving" person. I believe very firmly that this principle is primary, paramount, and nonnegotiable. The Holy Bible teaches that any money—or crop from a field—that comes to us must be "tithed." In accordance with that teaching, I've always given back to God ten percent of any money that's come to me.

I was taught this in my young years: "Every dollar you ever get: give ten percent to God, save another ten percent and invest it wisely, and live on the balance." If you can't live on eighty cents out of every dollar earned, then you're living too high! Scale down your living standard—or earn more money. You can! Trust God. Give Him His share first, and He'll more than repay you. My testimony is that God is a very generous God!

———◆———

The Rule of Reciprocity

The Bible carries a promise—that God will be merciful to us. It also teaches a power principle which appears over and over in the Bible, stated different ways:

- "If you do not forgive men their trespasses, neither will your Father forgive your trespasses" (Matt. 6:15).

- "The measure you give will be the measure you get" (Matt. 7:2).

- "Cast your bread upon the waters, for you will find it after many days" (Eccles. 11:1).

- "Whatever a man sows, that will he also reap" (Gal. 6:7).

Give a little, you get a little back. Give a lot, you get a lot back. This is the *law of proportionate return* that Jesus is teaching in these verses. . . . If you are critical, you can expect people to criticize you. If you gossip about people, you can be sure these same people are going to gossip about you. It is a law of life as real and unavoidable as the physical laws that control our world and our bodies.

—◇—

Are You Robbing God?

To neglect to share with those in need is a form of stealing too. God said centuries ago, "You have robbed me!" The people were shocked. It is bad enough to rob your neighbor but would a man rob God? "Wherein have we robbed thee?" they asked. And God's answer came back to jolt their greedy hearts: "In tithes and offerings" (Mal. 3:8).

God has told us again and again that He will give to humans the right to own property, the energy to accumulate wealth; but we have the responsibility to return to Him who keeps our heart beating ten percent of everything He allows to come into our hand. This is tithing. He promises that if we take our right and accept our responsibility, He will bless us far beyond our imagination: "Bring ye all your tithes into the storehouse and prove me [test me, try me!] and see if I will not open the windows of heaven and pour you out blessings so that there shall not be room enough to receive it" (Mal. 3:10).

◈

Look Around—and Lend a Hand

We are allowed in the providence of God to succeed not for selfish reasons but for unselfish purposes. There will be no lasting self-esteem produced by your successes unless you are dedicated to helping your neighbor.

The only joy of success is to know that you've increased your power and capacity to help others. Looking down the mountain, you can see to say, "Look! he's heading the wrong way!" "See! she's taking the wrong turn! She's headed toward a precipice!" "Oh! they are moving too slow; they'll be caught in a storm before they reach base camp. They must move faster." "Look out! they are moving too fast. The road ahead has loose rocks. They must move slowly, cautiously."

You've traveled the road, you've made the climb, you've had your near misses, your risks, your almost falls. Now you can be helpful to those who are still struggling to move up the mountain. The joy of being at the top of the mountain is the joy of reaching down to help others see and develop their possibilities.

—◆—

Give Back

Do you feel useless and unimportant? How generous have you been in sharing your self, your talents, your substance with the less fortunate? We have a God-given right to be rich but we also have a God-given responsibility to share with those who are in need. The right and the responsibility cannot be separated from each other without damaging our whole economic system. For this reason Christian countries have at the same time produced capitalists and great philanthropists. Take stock and see the hospitals, libraries, churches, schools, colleges, medical research centers, charitable foundations, international missions with hospitals and schools, and the like, that have been produced by Christian capitalism.

It is no sin to be a capitalist, but it is a sin to be selfish. It is no sin to be wealthy, but it is a sin to be greedy. It is no sin to work for profit, but it is a sin to exploit the unfortunate.

It is our God-given responsibility to share, voluntarily, cheerfully, compassionately, with those who are in need. And in this sense, our nation has always had a Christian conscience. If a neighbor down the street suffers great financial problems and is burdened with overwhelming medical bills, the community traditionally rises to its responsibilities and helps meet the need. No man needs to starve in a Christian land.

Winter's Cold

I never fail to remind new Christians who join our church that there are seasons in the spiritual life. For most people the beginning of the Christian life is a springtime experience. The icy sea of doubt is broken; a new life springs from a cold heart. No wonder people describe it by saying, "I've been born again!" This is the springtime season of the soul. When the Christian matures through the disciplines, there is growth, sometimes painful, in exposure to summer sun and wind, and finally the ripening of the fruit. The harvest season arrives and you offer to God the fruit of a life of service. And, strangely, it is usually after a period of fruitful service that the wintertime comes.

It is the shock of it that bothers us most. We never thought we would see those old doubts, those old sins, those old troubles again! But here they are back, knocking at the door once more. . . .

The truth is that every Christian passes through a wintertime in his spiritual pilgrimage. . . . There are times when the light flickers, the glow burns low, the zeal fades, desolateness sweeps over the soul, doubt flashes its frigid face across our wintry path. Music no longer stirs the heart. Worship no longer lifts the spirit. Sweet tears no longer come to visit the eye. Prayer—a foolish empty wind! The heart shivers in a cold cell of cynicism. . . . The window, once clean and sparkling, is covered with film. And you wonder whether you still love your wife, whether you still believe in God, and whether or not you are in the right profession.

Careful! This is the winter season of the soul! Make no rash, impulsive, far-reaching decisions. This is a dark night for the heart. This is a stormy season for your spirit.

---◆---

When Winter Strikes

Why do these seasons come? Sometimes I suspect through simple neglect. Carelessly we skip a church service, we neglect our daily devotions, we are too busy to read our Bible and pray, and we foolishly think we are none the worse because of our undisciplined spiritual life. I can neglect to water and feed the plants in my garden and they seem none the worse for it until, suddenly, one day I discover that they are withering in the sun! G. K. Chesterton once confessed that when he was a young man he decided to put "his religion in the drawer for a while and have a good time." He would remember where he had put it and when he was in the mood for it, he would go back and reclaim it. Years later he went back for it. He opened the drawer, but it was empty! Dry seasons are inevitable if we neglect the spiritual exercises. The only way to keep your religion is to keep using it. . . .

Sometimes a secret sin harbored in the heart is enough to cause our soul and our spiritual life to become barren and dry, just as a grain of sand in the gas line of a car causes power to fail. If there is spiritual power lost in your life, check your secret heart carefully.

What shall we do when the shivering season strikes the soul? Jesus gave a beautiful answer in a parable. "Ye ought always to pray and faint not." Like the widow who kept appealing to the judge, refusing to take no for an answer, so we, too, must unceasingly pray to God. "I will not let Thee go, O Lord, except Thou bless me."

God's Message of Hope

The darker the suffering, the brighter the message that the sender shares with everyone.

The principle is best illustrated by a sight I witnessed while flying over the Pacific Ocean. I thought I'd seen the wake of every possible boat or ship. . . .

Long or short, narrow or wide—it's always been a thrilling sight to me to look back and see the wake that's left behind. But flying over the ocean I saw a wake such as I've never seen before. I saw it from the window of a commercial jet. At first I thought the marks on the water were hidden reefs. But my companion said, "It looks like the wake of a vessel, but those lines are too far apart to be that!"

As we flew on, we could see that the lines were in fact moving closer together, the way a wake would look. And finally we saw the vessel that created the wake. What had made this mammoth wake? Was it an aircraft carrier? No. It was just a very slim, slender, black, short line in the water with a periscope piercing the surface.

I said, "It's a submarine!"

My companion said, "It is, at that."

It had just surfaced. And a submarine, when it surfaces after plowing through the depths, leaves a wake that is remarkable.

I tell you today: people who go through the deep waters of suffering leave a wide wake if they choose (and it is a choice) to trust and forgive. In spite of their suffering, they send a huge message of hope to the world.

APRIL 4

The Valley of the Shadow

Peace of mind comes to the person who feels the presence of God.

No one has put it better than the Psalmist: "Yea, though I walk through the valley of the shadow of death, I will fear no evil: for thou art with me." This simple sentence has calmed more nervous souls, comforted more lonely people, encouraged more timid hearts than all the tranquilizers and psychiatrists put together!

Nothing can stop the man who feels the presence of God in his life. Terror is like morning dew in a noonday sun. Fear is ice on summer seas. The tense, trembling, troubled heart becomes as placid and peaceful as water in an inland lake moments before the dawning of the day.

Don't trust the clouds—trust the sunshine. Don't set your compass by the flash of lightning—set it by the stars. Trust the sun—don't trust the shadows. Believe in your dreams—don't believe in your despairing thoughts. Have faith in your faith—and doubt your doubts. Trust in your hopes—never trust in your hurts.

◆

He Restoreth My Soul

Can you remember a night when you could not sleep? It seemed the day would never dawn. You finally rose from a bed that refused to give you comfort or rest. You walked out into the still black morning. You looked anxiously for the first stirring of creeping daylight but the morning star was still sleeping under the blanket of night. Around you an unlighted world huddled in the chilly shadows. Would daylight never come?

And then, out of the silent shadows, you heard a single note—the sweet, fresh, wide-awake note of a bird! And after a pause another note from another corner answered. The birds stirred. Note answered note. Song answered song until the wakening birds made the morning happy with music, as if singing a processional for the royal sun about to make its gallant entrance over the eastern hill. And the born-again morning finally came. Daylight was restored.

"He restoreth my soul." It is God's way of promising us that after a fitful night there will be a new day; after the storm, new calmness; after the night, a new day; and after the winter, a resurrected springtime.

—◆—

Transformed

Today the cross is the positive symbol of the happiest religion in the whole world. Persecuted? You and I can choose to be happy—anyway! For we believe that Jesus was resurrected on Easter morning! My personal conviction is this: Jesus Christ is alive this very moment!

What does Christ's persecution, crucifixion, and resurrection mean to us? It means that if we allow Christ to live in us, then it will be possible for us, also, to:

- Turn our problems into opportunities.

- Tackle our opportunities and succeed!

- Dream great dreams and make them come true!

- Switch from jealousy and self-pity to really caring about others who are much worse off than we are.

- Pick up the broken hopes and start over again!

- See great possibilities in those unattractive people!

- Become a truly beautiful person—like Jesus!

Look at Jesus Christ

Jesus Christ was the greatest mountain climber of all times. He climbed all the way to the top of the mountain of Calvary. And from that point He has been conquering the hearts of men and women for two thousand years. From His mountain peak, Jesus Christ won my heart.

But Jesus didn't have to climb that mountain—He could have stopped before He reached the top. Praying in the Garden of Gethsemane, Jesus said, "Father, Father, everything is possible for you. Take away this cup from me. Yet your will, not mine, be done" (Mark 14:36). He could have escaped the mob that arrested Him, but He didn't. He wasn't martyred, tricked, or cornered. He willingly sacrificed His life, for it was all part of the plan. Jesus knew what He had to do, and with joy He set His face to the cross!

Who killed Jesus? Nobody did. "Nobody takes my life from me," he said, adding, "I give it up!" So his death was not a murder, not an execution, and not a suicide—but a sacrifice. Suicide is the ultimate act of selfishness. Sacrifice is the ultimate act of self-giving love. What a Lord we have in Christ.

—◇—

The Perfect Portrait

And what kind of God do you see when you look at His image in Christ? You see first a God who guides. As a lad, I had a little boat which I pulled with a string around in circles in a large tank of water. God does not pull us like a boy pulls a boat tied on a string. I also recall the early spring days in Iowa when we would walk a mile home to our farm from the country school. The ditches along the country roads had been filled with drifting snow in the winter. The warm spring sun would melt the snow and create little streams in the ditches. We boys used to put a little twig in the stream at the schoolhouse and guide the little "boat" all the way home. Sometimes it would become snagged and with a long stick we would gently prod it loose and send it freely on its way again. God guides you with enthusiasm and intense interest when you give your life over to Him.

And all the while, He provides. "The Lord is my Shepherd, I shall not want," was David's faith. This is the grand image of God that we see in the perfect portrait of Him in Jesus Christ. For our Lord promised, "Ask, and ye shall receive. . . ." And again to assure us that God would not only guide but provide, Jesus said, . . . "Consider the lilies of the field, how they grow; they toil not, neither do they spin. And yet I say unto you, that even Solomon in all his glory was not arrayed like one of these. Wherefore, if God so clothe the grass of the field . . . shall he not much more clothe you, O ye of little faith? . . . Your heavenly Father knows that you have need of all these things" (Matt. 6:26–32).

A Man from Galilee

He had no "connections." He just didn't know the right people. He couldn't impress people by dropping big names. He couldn't be a name-dropper if He wanted to be. (Except to say that He and the Almighty were very good friends.) What kind of people was He attracted to? Not to the VIPs. Not to the lords of industry, politics, commerce, society, government, education, or religion.

What kind of people was He attracted to? To any person who could think big, believe big, and imagine big beautiful dreams.

A fisherman who was able to believe that he could be a somebody.

A diseased woman who dared to believe that she could be healed.

A whore who dared to think that she could be a lady.

A crooked politician who dared to believe that he could recover his lost dignity.

Why was He attracted to this kind of people? Because these were the only kind He could help! And these were the only kind of people who could help Him. He wanted to accomplish the impossible. He wanted to change the world. He believed that if He got the right people with the right spirit, He could succeed in changing the world. But they had to be beautiful believers—Possibility Thinkers.

—◆—

A Failed Plan?

When He found himself with His hands hammered to a wooden cross he turned his crucifixion into a wonderful opportunity to dramatically tell all the world for all time that there is no sin that God cannot forgive!

So He prayed, "Father, forgive them; for they know not what they do." And the cross has become a joyous symbol to remind the world that if God can forgive this depraved torture of an innocent Christ, He can forgive any sin. After He died some friends tenderly lifted Him down, gently wrapped His naked body, and put Him in a borrowed tomb.

"That's that!" thought the crowd which had finished its bloody deed. "Good riddance," thought His enemies. He had enemies. One evil that He could not tolerate was "insincere religion." He hit that hard and it got Him into trouble.

The crosses were taken down. Drifting sand would soon fill the holes. His body was dead and so was His "big idea," grandiose dream, and exaggerated talk. His followers were scattered. They were, frankly, scared stiff. Would they be next? No movement could be more obviously dead than His movement on that day. For He died. Leaving no manuscripts. No corporation. No property. No headquarters. Only a big idea that any man can do almost anything if he lives close to God and has enough faith.

This was His big idea.

And it seemed like His death proved Him wrong.

APRIL 11

—◆—

Turnaround

But then something happened.

Whatever it was, His crushed, defeated, broken teammates suddenly were inflamed with a greater faith than any band of human beings in the history of the human race has ever displayed.

For He appeared to them. Alive again! With a powerful message!—

"Of course there is a God! I saw Him!"

"Of course there is life after death! I have been there to give the answer once and for all!"

"Of course God hears and answers prayers!"

"Of course you can go out and change the world! All of this is possible!"

This was what He came back from his grave to tell them. And these cowardly followers became the bravest men history has ever seen. They came out of hiding and into the streets. One thing is sure: they were positive that they had seen their Teacher alive again. All were so positive of it that whereas they were too scared to even show their faces one day, they were out preaching from the street corners not many days later, not caring at all if they were killed themselves. "You people are drunk," someone said.

"Hardly, friend," they answered. "The truth is, this Christ who was killed is still alive! We saw Him. We talked to Him."

And these Impossibility Thinkers finally became the world's greatest Possibility Thinkers. Nothing could stop them. Nothing could keep them from succeeding. The spirit of their Possibility Thinking Master had at last completely caught hold of them. And they were changed men.

—◆—

Expansion Plans

They didn't realize it but this Possibility Thinker was about to solve His biggest problem. For He had one big problem on this earth. It seemed like an "impossible problem." He could only be one place at a time.

Someone said to me recently, "It's too bad He isn't around today. We could sure use Him." And they added sadly, "Why did He have to die anyway?"

"Die? He isn't dead," I answered. "It seems to me that His Spirit is very, very much alive today."

"He just got rid of His body," I suggested. Adding, "That was the biggest problem He faced, you know. He had a body so he could only be one place at a time. While He was in the north, He should have been in the south too. I'm sure He must have thought many times, 'I wish I had a million bodies. A million hearts. A million tongues. Two million hands. I wish I could be at a million places at the same time.'"

So He conceived of the brilliant scheme of getting His body out of the way, and sending His living Holy Spirit into the thinking brains of millions of people of every race, in every city, in every country, in the whole world! His way of getting to a million places at the same time!

Guess what? He is alive this very moment sending His messages into the minds of people. Your brain was deliberately designed to pick up God's spiritual signals in the form of ideas, impulses, and moods. Christ is busy this very moment sending out a message to you. It takes the form of a "possibility thought" in your mind. Listen to it! Respond to it! And Christ can live in you!

All Things Through Christ

Jesus Christ would love to be wherever you are. Christ can be there by coming into your thoughts, feelings, and actions. Let Christ come into your total being and

- *Words will come out of you* that will shock you.

  "Did I say that?" you will ask.

- *Ideas will shoot into your mind* that will amaze you.

  "Did I think of that?" you will ask.

- *Feelings will rise strongly within you* to care about people you didn't care about before.

  "That's not like me," you will confess.

- *Impulses will suddenly stir within you* to help the unfortunate and to change your own bad habits, and you will begin to realize that *Christ is actually living in you!*

And you will say, as another famous Jew said centuries ago, "I can do all things through Christ who strengthens me." Of course! Christ keeps sending strong possibility thoughts. In the face of overwhelming obstacles we "get a bright idea." We just cannot be defeated when we are in contact with this great living soul. We see opportunities all around us. Always. All the days of our life. "If any man is in Christ, he becomes a new creature. Old things are passed away, behold! All things are become new."

—◆—

God Needs Us

So Christ is living and working in this world.

He was living in the minds of the first American astronauts spinning in space.

Using the thinking minds and feeling hearts and strong wills of good men and women, He is teaching, healing, inventing, negotiating, forgiving, reassuring.

Wherever you are and whatever you do—if you have any contact at all with any other living human beings—you can be sure that Christ can use you and wants to live another life reincarnated within you. That is the supreme possibility of human life.

Christ has no hands but our hands to do His work today.
He has no feet but our feet to lead us on the way.
He has no tongues but our tongues to tell us how He died.
He has no help but our help to bring us to His side.

Christ Alone

Christ always tried to give a person's self-image a boost. When He met immoral people He never called them sinners. Never! "Follow me and *I will make you* into wonderful people," He said. One of the most despised members of His society was the Jew who was a tax-collecting tool of the Roman army of occupation. Such a man was Zaccheus. When Jesus met him, He might have judged him harshly. Instead, He sought to build this man's sense of self-love by offering to spend the night at this two-faced tax collector's house.

It is interesting that the only persons ever accused of being horrible sinners by Christ were the very narrow-minded, legalistic, hyperreligious people. "A generation of vipers," He called them. What did they do that was so hellish? *Under the guise of authoritarian religion, they destroyed man's sense of self-affection and self-worth.* Perhaps nothing destroys one's sense of self-respect more than the finger-pointing, wrist-slapping, fist-shaking religious authority which claims to speak in the name of God.

Dr. Samuel Shoemaker, a prominent American churchman, said, "Religion can never be the answer to human problems. All of the religions of the world are inadequate. Christ alone is the answer. Christ alone understands. Christ alone forgives. Christ alone eliminates your guilt. Christ alone saves and then assures you that you are God's child and the most wonderful person possible! Christ alone fills the human heart with love—joy—peace—self-confidence. No wonder a genuine Christian really loves himself."

—◆—

The Good Life

If you want to know what is meant by the good life, direct your attention to Jesus Christ. This was the good life incarnate.

What was life like for Him? Take a look at His last days on earth and you will see the secret of His satisfying life. Shortly before He died He said to His apostles, "I would that my joy might be in you and that your joy might be complete" (John 15:11). The good life, then, is a life that has an inner joy.

Then hear this: "Peace I leave with you, my peace I give unto you: not as the world giveth, give I unto you. Let not your heart be troubled, neither let it be afraid" (John 14:27). The good life is a life that has a deep undercurrent of profound peace.

The last words to fall from Christ's lips, as He hung and died under the Jerusalem sky, were short and simple, but triumphant: "It is finished" (John 19:30). He had carried out His divine mission. The good life is the awareness of fulfillment. For "every man's life is a plan of God." God has a plan for you. And the good life is the deep feeling that we are fulfilling God's plan and purpose in our life.

You Are Invited . . .

We have an invitation to sit at God's table, to receive salvation from our sins through Jesus Christ. This is the great invitation: "Come unto me, all you who labor and are heavy laden, and I will give you rest."

Listen to Him! How winsome! How warm! How welcoming! How wonderful!

This is God, inviting you—now! This is God, inviting you— who suffer with inner shame, and regret, and remorse; with hands that are not clean, hearts that are not pure, a mind that has been defiled, and a soul that is sick. This is for you! God is saying: "Come let us reason together. Though your sins be as scarlet, they shall be as white as snow. Though they be red like crimson, they shall be as wool."

The very name of Jesus is an invitation to life abundant and eternal. And we take this name and this gospel in vain. The Bible says that Jesus Christ is not dead—that He still lives. And I believe it. Jesus Christ is alive. He confronts the world and invites mankind to come and accept Him as Savior and Lord, but we smile politely and don't take Him too seriously. Mind you, when you do, your immortal soul is redeemed. Your destiny is secure. The Eternal becomes your God and God your Father!

—◆—

Do Something Beautiful for God

In a negative-thinking world, we are constantly surrounded by negative vibrations. The most positive person you meet still has his negative attitudes. No person is one-hundred-percent positive. We are emotionally conditioned to negativity by the world in which we live. How do we break these hypnotizing, negative chains? How do we liberate ourselves from the imprisonment of negative thinking? How do we say "No" to the negatives, the temptations that will rob us of our happiness?

Say "No!" by saying "Yes!" Eliminate the negatives by sowing positives. . . .

A perfect communication between two people isn't the type of relationship in which there are no fights, no arguments, no cross words. Perfect communication is when both persons are able to open up and actually tell each other how they feel with respect and mutual esteem. Not silence, but creative, constructive, respectful conversation is righteousness in communication.

So, we cannot claim that we are striving after righteousness by making a list of "don'ts" and trying to abide with them. Hungering and thirsting after righteousness must mean more than that! It must mean desiring to live the positive kind of life that will bear fruit and do something beautiful for God.

The Psalmist says that the *righteous* man shall be "like a tree planted by streams of water, that *yields its fruits in its season*, and its leaf does not wither. In all that he does, he prospers."

—◆—

Say "Yes!"

Righteousness comes through positive affirmations:

- "I'm a child of God!"

- "I'm God's idea, and God has only good ideas!"

- "I *want* to do it! I *can* do it! I *will* do it!"

- "I'm going to take chances!"

When you say "Yes!" you will be living and trusting in God's promises. When you attempt the impossible you will discover that you will be filled with excitement! Enthusiasm! Energy! Youth! Happiness!

Righteousness is attempting to accomplish some beautiful possibility. Win or lose—the attempt will build your self-esteem. Succeed or fail—you can be sure of this—you will be able to live with yourself and not be ashamed, which means you can be proud that you tried.

That's the joy! That's the deep satisfaction! That is the great reward!

—◈—

Why Say "No" to God?

If righteousness is so great, why isn't everybody pursuing it? What holds people back? Why do people say "No" to the good things? Why do they say "No" to God? . . .

First, people say "No" to God because *they do not know any better*. There are still a lot of people who are hung up on the idea that if you really get religion, really get converted, really get saved and become a Christian, you may go off the deep end and become a little nutty or kooky or freaky. There are others who have been turned off by contact with religious hypocrites or fanatics or—worse—by joyless, negative Christians. So these people steer away from religion, never realizing what a happy life they can have when they commit their whole lives to Him.

Dwight Moody used to say, "People have just enough religion to make themselves miserable; they cannot be happy at a wild party and they are uncomfortable at a prayer meeting."

How true it is! Many people have just enough religion to be miserable, but not enough to enjoy it. And so often this is because they have no idea what Christian life is really like. . . .

There is a second reason why some people say "No" to God: *They do not think they can say "Yes" to Him*. Lack of self-esteem holds them back. Their thinking is: "God is perfect and I surely know I am not; therefore, I do not think I should join up with Him." What these people don't realize is that God does not call us to be perfect; He just calls us to be willing! He doesn't expect us to be sinless, although He does expect us to say, "Lord, I am willing to try." It is far better to do some good imperfectly than to do nothing perfectly!

———◇———

Not Ready

Some people say "No" to God [because] *they think they are not quite ready*. They have projects that they have not started, projects that are half finished, telephone calls to make, unanswered letters to write. When they get their desks cleared and have a chance to think, probably then they will turn to God. But right now they are just too busy.

The trouble is, there may not be a "later on." Do it now! Do not let God wait. If you feel a positive, inspiring thought go through your mind today, there is only one way to answer it: "Yes, Lord."

Say it now. It is not going to hurt you. Right now, lay this book on your lap and say the words, "Yes, Lord." Repeat them out loud until they sound natural. "Yes, Lord! Yes, Lord! Yes, Lord!"

Do not be afraid of seeming overly dramatic or of being overly emotional; do not let any negative fear hold you back. Say it strongly, positively: "Yes, Lord." I predict that within an hour a positive thought will come into your mind. A positive mood will begin to creep over you. When that happens, do not say, "No." Say again, "Yes, Lord."

—◇—

Who Are the Kind People?

Without kindness the mighty are ruthless. Without kindness the emotionally stable are emotionally cold and hard. Without kindness the intelligent become arrogant. . . .

Who are the kind people? They are the *sensitive spirits*. Happy indeed is the heart which is sensitive to another's insecurity. Loving is he who offers reassurance to another's hostility, affection to another's loneliness, friendship to another's hurt, and apologies to all. Blessed are such sensitive souls, for they shall inherit the devotion and esteem of good people on this earth! . . .

The kind people are the sensitive spirits. They are the quiet people, through whom God can do so much. They are also those who are *willing to be third*. Happy, indeed, are the people who are willing to put Jesus first, others second, and themselves third in line. Richly rewarded in this life are those who learn the lesson of our Lord that if any man would be master, he should learn to be a servant:

- "Whoever would be great among you must be your servant, and whoever would be first among you must be your slave" (Matt. 20:26, 27).

- "He who finds his life will lose it, and he who loses his life for my sake will find it" (Matt. 10:39).

The kind people are the sensitive spirits, they are the quiet people, and they are willing to be third. But most importantly, they are *God-shaped, Christ-molded* people.

Unholy Pride

Only when you and I reach those depths of despair are we then on the way to joy, because God particularly pours out His blessings upon those who know how much they need Him. The *promise* is joy. The *principle* is to ask God for help, admit we cannot do it alone. The *problem*, of course, that stands in the way of our crying out to God is the problem of an *unholy pride*.

There is such a thing as a holy pride—self-esteem and self-respect represent a healthy pride in ourselves as God's loved and redeemed creation. But arrogance and vanity result from an unholy pride that says, "Get out of my way, I want to do it myself"—like a stubborn small child refusing a loving parent's help.

"Blessed are the poor in spirit, for theirs is the kingdom of heaven." And so you and I come to a time when we stop playing games, putting on false fronts. We reach a point in life when we know that we are spiritually bankrupt. It is at this point that we kneel before our Lord and say, "God, I want to be born again. I want a new life. I want a joyful Christ to come and live in me. Oh God, I turn my life over to You." . . .

Think about it. Before Jesus can comfort us, before He can help us and heal us, we must have the attitude that we are *willing* to be helped! He cannot make us happy unless we *want* to be happy.

So are you willing to be helped? Do you want to be happy? Are there some areas in your life where you are lacking and need some help?

—◇—

Sacrificial Pride

There's no success without sacrifice. By the cross approach I mean self-denial. There's no success without self-denial. Yet, as I study successful persons whose lives reflect a movement from one peak to another, I see something deeper than sacrifice, self-denial, and struggle. The real synonym for the word "cross" is the word "humility."

What does humility mean? Is it the opposite of pride? Not necessarily. True humility is a form of pride. It is what I call sacrificial pride. And you're never going to climb to the top of the mountain of success unless you have enough humility to do two things: (1) admit to yourself that you need help, and (2) ask someone else to help you. No person can achieve success alone. It's impossible. Even an artist in an attic has to have somebody willing to buy his paintings.

The voice of humility says, "I need help."

Healthy pride and honest humility are the heads and tails of the same coin.

——◇——

Resisting Help

A few months ago my wife and I were sitting in a hotel breakfast room when a man came in with his two small sons and sat at the adjoining table.

"What did you do with your socks?" the father asked one of his sons. The tone hinted of an appropriate parental rebuke. The dialogue continued. I couldn't hear the conversation, but then the father spoke, not softly, but firmly, "Are you making it hard for people to help you?!" . . .

The question haunted me. Do hurting people make it hard for people to help them? If so, do they know it? And if so, why would hurting people hurt the people who are trying to help them?

Remember the lady . . . who said to me, "The hurt that pained me the most through it all was not what he did to me so much as having to see what he was doing to himself. It hurts so badly to see someone you love hurting himself and refusing all efforts to rescue him from a path that leads to shame and ruin"?

The deeper question is, Why do people reject, resist, or fail to recognize all the help that's available?

In a summary sentence, here's my answer to that crucial question: the wounded heart may instinctively yield to overwhelming negative emotions. And that's where we consciously, or unconsciously, make it extremely difficult for people to help us.

——◇——

Dare to Ask for Help

How many people fail because they don't set priorities wisely? And how often is a positive idea denied top priority because we don't want to ask for the help we know we need or because we don't want to share the credit? "Pride goes before destruction" (Prov. 16:18).

Dare to ask for help! Smart people who are humble enough to admit that they need help—and are willing to share the power and glory of their success—will find amazing support from wonderful strangers. Here's the exciting promise of the first of the Beatitudes of Jesus: "Blessed are the poor in spirit for theirs is the kingdom of heaven" (Matt. 5:3).

APRIL 27

Christ Strengthens Me

"I can do all things—*through Christ* who strengthens me." And how does Christ strengthen us? Does He come here with meat and bones and hair and blood to stand at our side? Yes, He does. For His spirit enters into human beings whose lives He controls positively. So when I listen to the advice of smarter people, Christ strengthens me. When I accept help from people who can do a better job than I can, Christ strengthens me. I seek the counsel of experts in law, finance, taxes, and marketing. They are good people, smart people, people in whose lives Christ is living to be my strength!

This means I will not be defensive under constructive criticism from good counsel. This may be Christ coming to correct me! I will have the attitude that some people are smarter than I am; I will have the attitude that some people know something that I don't; I will have the attitude that there are people who are more skillful and gifted and creative than I am. So I shall be open to them, rather than closing my mind and my life to the contributions they can make.

—◆—

The Paths of Righteousness

"He guides me on the right track for His name's sake," is the way C. C. Briggs translates the classic line from the Twenty-third Psalm. What remarkable confidence, what superior calmness, what extraordinary faith are expressed here! Whoever the poet is, he is very positive in his thinking, and steady in his soul: "He guides me on the right track."

Precisely, what is his faith? It is this—although he travels a long and perilous journey, he enjoys the presence of a Guide who keeps him from taking a dangerous turn off the right road. "Thy rod and Thy staff they comfort me." . . .

Is it possible for a human being to be guided by supernatural wisdom in the decision-making moments of life? Christians, of course, claim that God is a living, invisible, personal Spirit who penetrates our mental consciousness and guides us. So we constantly pray for divine guidance when decisions must be made. We realize that the possibility of human error is almost infinite. Is this an opportunity that I am passing by? How shall I interpret these facts? How shall I judge this man? What tactics shall I take in this struggle? We often need the wisdom of Solomon! "He guides me on the right track." Ah, that is what we really need!

The hill country of Judea is wooded, rough terrain. . . . But the shepherd knows the hills and is able to guide his flock safely through dangerous territory. For he knows what lies on the other side of the hill. "He shall feed his flock like a shepherd . . . and gently lead those that are with young." So this Psalmist believed that as a shepherd is able to guide sheep safely through perilous and uncharted territory, so God is surely guiding his life on the right track.

———◆———

Designed by God

I have many things in my office. There is a desk, a chair, a divan, a painting, a pen-and-pencil set, a typewriter, and a radio. Of all these things in my office only the radio is able to pick up messages and music out of the air. Why is the radio alone so gifted? The answer is incredibly simple—because the radio was *designed* to pick up messages from the air. Because there is music on the air waves and we want to pick it up we design an instrument to accomplish this purpose. And so, God wanted one creature in His creation that would be able to pick up His divine messages and enjoy the music of the universe! So He created the human being with a mechanism designed to pick up spiritual signals. We call that mechanism the soul.

God penetrates our consciousness with sudden inspirations, unexpected brilliant moments, and unexplainable illuminations. There are high moments in our lives when our minds are strangely alert, wide awake, amazingly fertile, startlingly productive, and ideas flow in a delightful and thrilling torrent of dynamic thought. We are shocked at our own extraordinary spiritual aliveness. How do you explain these times? When walking at night on an unfamiliar road, you are not sure of your path in the blackness until suddenly the clouds split to let a full moon illuminate the world around you clearly. You can see trees sleeping in the night, mountains standing strong around you, until the shifting clouds slide back across the golden moon and you are left in the dark again. But the light has shined long enough for you to get your bearings and you are able to move ahead with confident footing. So in an unexpected moment, God's Spirit illuminates our minds.

—◇—

Still Skeptical?

Still there are those who do not see the hand of God in human affairs! How can we make them see it? How do you convince an illiterate person that the book placed in his hands actually contains a message? Or how can you prove to a person born deaf, dumb, and blind that he is surrounded by sounds, colors, music, and light? Or how do you teach a man who has lived all his life in a cave that he actually has a shadow? He will not believe it unless he is able to get out of his darkness and stand in the sunshine. . . .

To us who have felt the guidance of God in our life it is all very, very plain. So I say to you who struggle with skepticism, if you were to park your car in the parking lot of our church and saw before you a pile of lumber, a heap of rocks, sheets of glass, long strips of aluminum, and beams of steel, and suddenly, without a single human being intervening, you saw the wood float into the sky and join together, and at the precise moment beams of steel spontaneously soar into proper place, followed by flying strips of aluminum, then sheets of glass that slid through the sky like flying carpets, and everything finding its perfect place in a framework that was spontaneously erecting itself until before your very eyes you saw this modern sanctuary rise, take shape, and put itself together—what would you think? You would assume that there was some invisible intelligent force at work, planning everything and putting everything together!

It is thus that we view our universe, which is far more beautiful, far more complex, and far more orderly. No human being has ever laid claim to its design or its erection. There has been no human intervention whatsoever. Yet it is here, beautiful and organized.

MAY 1

———◇———

Surrender

How are we guided? The answer is no secret. Surely God speaks to us through the Bible! Those who read it quietly and prayerfully find God's guidance. And prayer is still the mysterious experience where we tune our minds to the celestial wavelength and ask God to guide us. In addition, there are thousands of people who will testify that in the quietness of worship God entered into their consciousness to illuminate them.

But I would suggest that the real secret of receiving divine guidance is deeper than Bible reading, prayer, or worship. The key word is *surrender*. Surrender your sins, your self-centered desires, and your life to Jesus Christ. Surrender your mind to the Holy Spirit. Are you sure you want guidance? Would you take it if He gave it?

Do you know how to catch a dove? It is interesting that in the New Testament the dove is the symbol of the Holy Spirit. And the Holy Spirit is God who enters into our mental consciousness. Hundreds of thousands of visitors to the San Juan Capistrano Mission in Southern California try to catch the white doves that flock in the ancient mission. You may reach out with your hand, fingers open, and just as you are about to grasp the feet of the dove, it flaps its wings and flies away. So you try again. You reach out with your hand cautiously, slowly, furtively, and just as you are about to grab the bird, it escapes again. The secret is this: Simply extend your hand. Hold it out straight in front of you. Open your palm. Wait quietly. And the dove will come and rest right in the middle of your hand. Surrender your soul, your mind, your spirit that way to God. And He will take over your life and guide you.

God's Peace

We take God's promises in vain. No wonder our trembling world is so frightened! Let's have an honest understanding. God is not the inventor of fear. He is not responsible for our worry, fear, and anxiety. It's our own fault. If we took God's promises seriously, we would mount up with wings like eagles, run and not be weary, walk and never faint.

For instance, take the man who can't get to sleep at night and tosses in his bed. First, he begins to worry that he might not fall asleep. And then he thinks that if he doesn't get to sleep, he's not going to have the strength to do his job. He is going to crack up, he fearfully imagines, and his career will be ruined. So his imagination works overtime and before he knows it, he has fabricated a terrifying ghost that haunts his mind, and robs him of the joy of living! What he needs is spiritual therapy. Let him read some of God's wonderful promises of peace and love and power and in quietness of mind he will rest in a natural sleep. Quietly, gently, tenderly, let the promise of God fall softly and sweetly into your tense, tight mind: "Thou wilt keep him in perfect peace whose mind is stayed on thee." "Peace I give unto you—let not your heart be troubled, neither let it be afraid." "I am the Lord your God." Reach for your Bible, friend, and underline the positive promises of God and trust them. Indescribable peace is bound to follow!

—◇—

Wait—and Work

Probably nothing is more difficult than to keep waiting, working, plodding, and maintaining patience through dark times. But we must. And in God's good time, hope and help will come our way. Oftentimes someone's unexpected, off-the-cuff comment or curt answer to an important question can be the breakthrough to a new emotional sunrise.

Henry Ford was born on a farm, left the farm at the age of sixteen, and got a job as a mechanic in Detroit. Then he became a fireman in the Detroit Edison Company and worked his way up until he became the chief engineer. Of course, Edison was just a big name to him. When Thomas Edison was visiting the company, Henry Ford told himself that if he ever got close enough to this famous inventor, he would ask him one question. Ford got the chance in 1898. He stopped Edison and said, "Mr. Edison, may I ask you a question? Do you think gasoline is a good fuel source for motor cars?" Edison had no time for Ford; he simply said yes and walked away. And that was it. But that answer turned Ford on. Henry Ford made a commitment. It was in 1909, eleven years later, that he turned out the Tin Lizzy. . . .

"Those who wait on the Lord shall renew their strength." The Lord might strengthen you through some person, or a chance meeting. It may come through someone God uses to encourage you. I know this is true because there have been times when I needed to be encouraged. And there have been other times when God used me to give encouragement to someone else. "Wait on the Lord." Remain in touch with God through prayer.

—◇—

Just a Natural Transition

Every institution, every individual, every job has its ages, passages, periods, eras; we have to be careful to hold on. When the brownout is only a brownout and not a burnout, the power will come back on. When there is a temporary overload on the emotional system, we must rest, wait upon the Lord, and the new dawning will come.

The most dangerous thing in the world is to make an irreversible negative decision during a brownout time. Don't sell your real estate because there is no electricity in the building. It's just a brownout, not a burnout. Never cut a dead tree down in the wintertime. I remember one winter my dad needed firewood, and he found a dead tree and sawed it down. In the spring to his dismay new shoots sprouted around the trunk. He said, "I thought sure it was dead. The leaves had all dropped in the wintertime. It was so cold that twigs snapped as surely as if there were no life left in the old tree. But now I see that there was still life at the taproot." He looked at me and said, "Bob, don't forget this important lesson. Never cut a tree down in the wintertime." Never make a negative decision in the low time. Never make your most important decisions when you are in your worst mood.

Wait. Be patient. The storm will pass. The spring will come. New feelings will come over you, and they will be positive. Keep waiting affirmatively and positively in prayer for God's strength to return.

◆

When I Face a Storm in Life

You never promised, Lord, that I would be forever sheltered from stormy times in my life. You have promised that the sun will outlast the storms.

You issue the grand command from outer space and the renegade storm clouds break up, scatter, and flee like hoodlums furtively racing from the streets, back to their hidden lairs in some forbidding alley. The bright stars come out to laugh again, like little children returning once more to safe streets for happy play.

The sky clears. A huge, yellow moon sails once more calm and serene through the silent skies.

Even as you restore peace after the storm, so will you bestow a renewed calm to my troubled mind through your peace-instilling presence that is surrounding me now.

Your quiet and calming spirit is flowing within me now. My fear is gone!

Thank you, Lord! Amen.

◇

Our Response to Trouble

What must you do with your trouble? Sir Harry Lauder, a great Scottish comedian, received the tragic news that his son was killed in the First World War. He wrote these penetrating lines: "In a time like this there are three courses open to a man. He may give way to despair, sour upon the world, and become a grouch. He may endeavor to drown his sorrow in drink, in a life of waywardness and wickedness . . . or he may turn to God!"

These are the three choices open to you.

If you use your head, there is only one choice that makes any sense. Turn to God! Years later you will testify that once you were stopped in your tracks by what appeared to be an impossibly cruel mountain that blocked your path. You were mercilessly forced to climb it with bleeding hands and a breaking heart, until you reached the summit and there you found, hidden behind the rugged peak, the greenest little pasture encircling a heaven-pure mountain lake! The greenest pastures I have seen have been in the terrible mountain ranges—precious pockets painfully gouged out by grinding glaciers centuries before.

Let your troubles lead you to Christ, and they will prove to be the best friends you ever had!

Allow Trouble to Lift You

Truly, we learn courage when we face danger; we learn patience when we endure suffering; we learn tenderness when we taste pain; we learn to prize true friends when false ones forsake us; we treasure health when illness strikes and we learn to prize freedom when we are in danger of losing it! Without trouble we would be like plants that have sprouted, grown, and been nurtured in the overprotected shelter of a hothouse, too tender ever to live in the open!

We have matured as Christians when we learn that there is no progress without pain; there is no conversion without crises; there is no birth without painful travail; there is no salvation without agonizing repentance and no Easter without a Good Friday! There is no service without suffering. . . .

So you are having trouble? You feel cheated and abandoned by God? Remember: the eagle stirs up the nest in order that the young might learn to fly! Your trouble may be your greatest opportunity!

Go down to the beach and watch the mountainous waves come crashing in and you will see two ways to meet a wave. The frightened, timid soul sees the monster wave looming, mounting, threatening. He turns, stumbling through the foamy shallows, and being too slow, he is overtaken, upset, flattened and sent sputtering in the surf by the liquid mountain. But farther in the deep you see a skillful rider of the surf who watches carefully the wave as it builds, swells, rises, and instead of running from the wave, he rides it! Instead of being flattened, he is lifted! Instead of being made low, he is raised high and carried far!

—◆—

Let Your Problem
Lead You to God

No problem leaves you where it found you. Read this affirmation out loud: "I will be a different person when this problem is past. I will be a wiser, stronger, more patient person; or I will be sour, cynical, bitter, disillusioned, and angry. It all depends on what I do with this problem. Each problem can make me a better person or a worse person. It can bring me closer to God, or it can drive me away from God. It can build my faith or it can shatter my faith. It all depends on my attitude. I intend to be a better person when this problem leaves me than I was when it met me."

There are vast untapped resources of faith and talent that can only be discovered in adversity!

—◇—

Change for the Better

You'll be a different person by the time your dark days pass. The future will be a better place if you become a better person because of your predicament.

How can adversity change you for the better? *Look* at who and where you are and where you want to go. *Learn.* You've made mistakes. Every single human has; no person is perfect. *Lean* on the best counsel you can find. Be genuinely humble. *Lift* others. All around you today—and in all of your tomorrows—there are human beings who are in bad straits. Turn your scars into stars. Teach others what you've learned the hard way.

What you do with your problem is far more important than what your problem does to you.

◈

Let Go and Let God

As children bring their toys
with tears for us to mend,
I brought my broken dreams to God,
because He was my Friend.
But then, instead of leaving Him in peace to work alone,
I hung around and tried to help
with ways that were my own.
At last I snatched them back and cried,
"How can You be so slow?"
"My child," He said, "what could I do?
You never did let go."

God Can Turn Your Hurt Inside Out

I have toured royal palaces around the world, but the Royal Palace in Tehran, Iran, is something else! There isn't anything like it, to my knowledge, anywhere in the world.

You step into the Royal Palace, and the grand entrance is resplendent with glittering, sparkling glass. For a moment you think that the domed ceilings, side walls, and columns are all covered with diamonds . . . until you realize that these are not diamonds or cut glass; they are small pieces of mirrors. The edges of a myriad of little mirrors reflect the light, throwing out the colors of the rainbow! A mosaic of mirrors! Spectacular!

You'll never believe how this happened. When the Royal Palace was planned, the architects sent an order to Paris for mirrors to cover the entrance walls. The mirrors finally arrived in their crates. When they took the crates apart, all the broken pieces fell out! They were all smashed in travel! They were going to junk them all when one creative man said, "No, maybe it will be more beautiful because the mirrors are broken."

So he took some of the larger pieces and smashed them, and then he took all the little pieces and fitted them together like an abstract mosaic. If you see it, you will note that it is an enormous distortion in reflections, and it sparkles with diamond-like rainbow colors.

Broken to be more beautiful!

Do you have a hurt?

If you do, turn it over to God, and He will turn it inside out.

———◈———

Transforming Trust

Trust God, and somehow, through someone, sometime, or some way, God will reconnect with your stumbling, struggling soul! Suddenly a door opens, and you will not feel abandoned anymore. That is real salvation! A brave new idea will emerge. Opportunities will rise out of your adversities. Strangers will enter your life to become new and best friends. A renewing faith will stir and grow within you. Miracles will be conceived and born out of grueling mysteries.

God has succeeded! He has achieved His glorious goal to make you into a true person, a trusting human, a powerful spiritual being.

Hurts? They still happen. But you will look into the dazzling darkness of God and know that something good will come from this!

Your cross will turn into your crown.

You will understand, "Life's not fair, but God is good!"

Now liberated from the imprisoning mental attitude that demands provable reasons for every element of faith, you become a truly whole and spiritually healthy human. The chains of cynicism are broken. Your mind is open to reach exciting possibilities even before they are probabilities. Your thinking becomes moldable, pliable, and receptive to the greatest idea ever to enter the human consciousness: there is a loving, caring God after all!

You have embraced a new lifestyle! It's called living in faith. Yes, the mystery becomes a miracle. You will never be abandoned again, for you are mentally, spiritually, and emotionally connected with your Creator.

—◆—

One Man's Faith

[Former baseball player] Dave [Dravecky told me] ..., "You know, life isn't fair. People can't expect always to see things peaches and cream and rosy. There are going to be times when we have a setback, but through trust in Jesus Christ we can have the peace to be content in the midst of the storm and that's what I experienced during that period of time [when I was fighting cancer]—that peace in the midst of the storm."

Dave's faith really taught me a lot. I responded to his comments, "So your trust in Jesus Christ didn't change the situation as much as it changed your attitude toward it. Would that be correct?"

"Most definitely. I had two choices. One choice was to give in to the despair to the point where I would not be able to endure this. My other choice was to put my faith and trust in Jesus Christ who was in control of my life. I decided to choose the latter path and enjoy what I was going through even though it may have been difficult. In retrospect, it has been a wonderful journey. It's been a blessing from God." ...

Dave's story is detailed in an exciting book entitled *Comeback* (Zondervan). In the book Dave made this statement: "Life's not fair, but let's not confuse life with God." ...

God is good. He doesn't create the problems—He redeems them. He doesn't make the mistakes—He fixes them. He doesn't cause cancer. He heals. He doesn't kill dreams or bodies. He gives life. He gives the big picture—the ability to see beyond this temporal setback to a glorious comeback!

You can be a living, loving testimony that life's not fair—but God is good!

When I Cannot Sleep

O God, around me an unlighted world huddles in chilly shadows. Will daylight never come? I wait for the morning calm—for the morning peace after a night of unrest.

Now, out of the silent shadows, I wait for the sweet, fresh, wide-awake note of a bird, for the awakening birds that will make the morning happy with music.

The long awaited sunrise is near. Daylight will soon be restored! The fitful night will give way to a new day filled with possibilities!

It's always sunrise, sometimes, somewhere! After every retreating storm there follows, on golden paths of sunlight, a returning, refreshing, renewing peace. After bleak and barren winter, the springtime always blossoms with fresh fragrance.

So until the first bird sings, I will enjoy this quiet moment of unsleeping solitude. I shall quietly rest and relax knowing I am protected from unwelcome interruptions.

We are alone, together, Lord. What surprises are you planning for me tomorrow? Amen.

—◇—

Embrace Change

Don't fear change. Welcome it as an opportunity! If change is a great problem, it is also a grand human hope. One word, one illustration, one idea can transform the whole complexion and the destiny of our life. I see this happening constantly. Some positive idea falls unexpectedly on the mind and changes forever the destiny of an entire family. Thank God we are not created to be rigid, nonchanging objects of marble, granite, or steel!

Not a Problem—an Opportunity

God is going to give you a problem, and that will be your opportunity. He will give you challenges. That will be your mountain. That is God's greatest gift to you. Face your mountains instead of cutting out or coasting. You'll experience the greatest joy of life: the joy of self-esteem that comes when you know you did what you had to do.

Every time one door closes, another door opens.

—◇—

No Time? No Excuse!

Before you turn down an invitation or an opportunity because you are too busy, analyze in depth your reasoning. You may not even be thinking. You may only be feeling. The truth is we all can find time for almost anything we really want to do. When something of overpowering importance comes your way, it is amazing how you can change your plan, shift your schedule, and cut out of your life activities which you thought were so important the day before. Are you sure you don't have the time? Perhaps you are basically afraid of involvement or failure. Perhaps you are fatigued. And in your depression it may be your negative emotions talking as you mutter, "I can't—I'm too busy." Remember, you may continue to feel weary until you say "Yes," and try. You will continue to be tired as long as you are unexcited about anything. And the way to get excited about anything is to get involved.

—◆—

Loaded with Opportunities

There was a lady who telephoned and asked to see me. She had been an unbeliever most of her life until the year before. Her reason for calling was that she had terminal cancer and wanted to see me. She lived in a tiny apartment just a few miles from my office. She couldn't have weighed more than eighty pounds. She was skin and bones. I sat next to her bedside and looked into her eyes. What beauty! Her eyes twinkled! They were so youthful-looking, too!

"Thank you for coming, Dr. Schuller," she said. "You brought faith into my life. I'm not afraid now. I know where I am going. Your Possibility Thinking has changed my attitude toward my sickness. I was bitter and angry at the world for so long. I was afflicted with self-pity and all these negative emotions until I turned them over to the Lord. That's when I thought about new possibilities for me. What could I possibly do for others in my condition? And I decided that I would try to minister to all the people who came to call on me. So, before anyone comes to visit I say a little prayer:

Dear God,
Help me to do something for them.
Help me to cheer them up!

And do you know what? These have been the most exciting weeks of my life. When people come, I share the love of God with them and they leave knowing God really cares for them. Isn't that wonderful?"

God never lets anything happen to you unless it is loaded with opportunities.

◇

Courage Is a Decision

The truth is that courage isn't a gift. Courage is a *decision!* Courage is not the absence of fear, it is the presence of a calling— a dream that pulls you beyond yourself. Hence it is something you can never lose. It is always something that you can choose. So, choose it today!

I have it!
My fears are going, going, gone!
I feel a mysterious, calm, quiet, tranquil assurance
rising deep within my being.
This remarkable spirit of courage is overpowering me.
It is the very presence of God working peace at the core
of my invisible soul.
Thank you, Lord. All my fears are gone. What a relief!
Amen.

——◇——

A Cry for Help

What is your problem? Is it a terminal diagnosis? Have you lost your job? Has your company folded? Has your husband left you? Your wife? Have your children turned against you?

Whatever it is, I urge you to learn from Possibility Thinking experts. They did it—so can you! They felt their rage, their anger, their hurt, their pain. Some of them got mad at God for a while. But they all reached a point where they were able to get down on their knees and ask God for the ability to do the best with what they had left.

I promise you, God always honors those kinds of requests. He will always respond to a cry for help—especially a call for courage.

Be bold! Courage isn't feeling free from fear; courage is facing fears you feel!

Choose the Right God

Get acquainted with the God and Father of our Lord Jesus Christ. Discover how He hears and answers prayer. Find out how He listens, and loves, and lifts. Discover how quietly He guides, guards, and undergirds! Then, like all the truly free people of the past centuries, you will find the Lord to be your God. . . .

Somehow we must learn that what we need most of all today are not more new things. We have enough gadgets now to enslave us. We find ourselves losing our freedom to the tyranny of things: The house says, "Repair me." The car shouts, "Wash me." The clothes cry out and demand, "Press me." We are already slaves to things.

Nor do we need new ideas. Some would-be solver of national and international problems thinks that what we need are some fresh imaginative ideas to solve man's problems. Secretly it is hoped that a brilliant new creative idea will pop up in some super-intellectual brain that will guide the world to everlasting peace.

The truth is that the big wonderful idea has already been thought of. What we need is not the discovery of new things or new ideas, but a rediscovery of the grand and glorious revelation to humanity two thousand years ago. My insecure friend, follow Christ, who came to lead humanity to the only true God.

God has spoken. He has drawn the curtain. He has opened the door. He has allowed us to catch a glimpse of Himself in the quiet tall Stranger of Galilee who hangs limp on a Roman cross. He, the wounded God, is the personification of the big idea that can save our world and give you the inner security you crave.

—◇—

Heed God's Warnings

It is high time we learned to take God's warnings seriously. This advice is imperative to anyone who wants to live the good life.

Near Forest Home, high in the California mountains, are beautiful falls. At the foot of these falls is a sign, posted there by the rangers. It says, simply, that the trail ahead is dangerous. It warns that the way to the top is precarious and has often been fatal. "Don't be next!" is the solemn slogan that summarizes the warning. Still, there are the adventurous souls who will climb to the top of the falls. There is no law against it. You are free to explore. You may challenge the trail. But if you are injured on the way, the rangers and the State of California are not responsible!

We tend to confuse warnings with threats. By mistake, threats are cruel manipulations by those who would control us. Warnings are signals to alert us to dangers that could harm us. "Before you take down the fences," G. K. Chesterton wrote, "ask why they were put up in the first place." Now it is natural that we do not want to hear and heed the divine warnings. Warnings are not happy sounds. No wonder we like to ignore them.

Discover the Right Prayer

A friend was having a problem with a competitor, and he was experiencing all kinds of negative emotions. I suggested he pray about it.

"What do I pray?" he asked. "Do I pray that the guy will succeed?"

"Well, I don't know. Just pray that God will tell you what to pray. Ask God what to pray for," I responded.

A week later, my friend told me, "I woke up at two o'clock in the morning, and I had the prayer."

"What was it?"

He told me this was the prayer:

Dear God, make that person into exactly the person you want him to be and cause his business to develop just the way you would like to see it develop. Amen.

My friend continued, "That just completely cured me. Now, if that guy's business succeeds, I can't possibly be angry about it. I know God wants it to grow." He was very sincere.

If you have a hurt and have prayed about it, but your prayer hasn't helped, then you may have prayed the wrong prayer. Instead, start by asking God what you ought to pray about.

—◇—

Trouble Redeemed

So often trouble is only a part of the painful growing process like a seed buried alive by a seemingly merciless fate under suffocating ground in a windowless grave, until in supreme agony it ruptures into a new life! This death, burial, pain, is not trouble! It is the travail of new birth! "Unless a grain of wheat fall into the ground and dies, it remains alone; but if it dies, it produces much grain" (John 12:24).

When trouble breaks your heart and makes your knees buckle, and forces penitent tears from eyes sealed in prayer to Almighty God, then trouble may turn out to be the redeeming agony before new birth!

Just what kind of people do you think we would be if we never had any trouble! For we build hard muscles in heart and body when we lift heavy loads. Tough times make calluses that may someday save our hands from bleeding!

—◇—

Impatient Dreamers

What is the single quality that more than any other identifies those who succeed? It is patience. Impatient dreamers will look for painless shortcuts and cheap discounts on the price of success! And failing to spot the expedient paths, unknowing, impatient dreamers will too often, too easily, and too painfully turn away from the divine dream. Later, when it's too late, they will discover that in choosing the painless, easy road they were in fact going down a primrose path to boredom, shame, emptiness, failure, poverty. If only they had not been afraid of the discipline that the dream demanded!

> The people who win in life are the people who have harnessed the power of patience. You can move a mountain, Christ said—but He didn't say how long it would take.

————◇————

You Can Count On Me

Jeb Stuart was a loyal follower of General Robert E. Lee. He was a courageous officer and a man of integrity who always signed his letters to the general, "You can count on me, [signed] Jeb."

Frankly, that's the commitment I've made to my God who gives me positive ideas. I have prayed, "If you will entrust the dream to me, Lord, *you can count on me!* I won't let it fly away. I'll do something with it. I will give it the best that I can!"

Courage? Yes. Integrity? Absolutely! I spell courage I-N-T-E-G-R-I-T-Y, for courage is really *honesty*. When you see someone who's operating with real courage, they're actually exhibiting integrity. They have to do what they're doing or they would be disloyal. I hope you will come to believe, as I do, that our dreams are *entrusted* to our care and keeping by God—with the obligation to turn an idea into creative action. Then, as an honest trustee, you will be so motivated by integrity that you'll have no place for fear.

—◆—

Fill Me!

*O Lord, like the thirsty deer which goes
to drink from the mountain spring;
like the growing flower which turns hungrily
to the satisfying sun;
like the empty pitcher which is carried to the
fountain to be filled;
so I come, O God, knowing
that in this time of prayer
my soul will be filled
with your love and your truth.
Thank you!
Amen.*

———◇———

Untapped Potential

Jesus Christ predicted—no, promised—that within each and every human being fantastic potential is waiting to be discovered and developed.

He proclaimed these powerful words: "The Kingdom of God is within you" (Luke 17:21). This means that there's an Eternal Creative Force within you. Mind and matter are alive with an energy that can be tapped and channeled to joyful creativity. See and seize it in science, in art and literature, in interpersonal relationships, in positive emotional power.

The power that we call God is designed to flow into, and through, the personalities and personal spiritual powers of human beings. When this dynamic divine energy is ignited within the human personality, the creative energy of the eternal God comes alive within us and we begin to experience and express phenomenal achievements; we begin to make a beautiful difference in our world. Then we become truly *wonderful*—yes, *full* of *wonder*— persons. "I wonder how she did it?" "I wonder how he made it?" That's living in the kingdom of God.

—◆—

Redesigned by Jesus Christ

There were some tough, crude, unschooled fishermen who ran into a fellow years ago. He put His hand on their shoulders and said, "Follow me and I will make you fishers of men!" It was their moment of inspiration. When they were discouraged and felt they didn't amount to anything, He said, "You are the salt of the earth. . . . You are the light of the world." More than anything they knew that they could be persons in a world of nonpersons. That great inspirer was a wonderful Jew who lived two thousand years ago. His name was Jesus Christ. What a great Possibility Thinker! Draw close to Him. Catch His spirit and you will never be the same again. Let Jesus Christ redesign your self-image. Tomorrow morning try this prayer by Norman Grubb:

Good morning, Christ.
I love you!
What are you up to today? I want to be part of it!
Thank you, God.
Amen!

Salt and Light

"You are the salt of the earth" (Matt. 5:13). Salt adds spice to the taste. Salt replaces boredom with excitement. You become the subtle and sensational force that brings fresh flavor and delightful fragrances into the drab, dreary, mental climate around you. And salt preserves as well. Your personality restores the joy of living to human existence and endurance.

"You are the light of the world" (Matt. 5:14), Jesus added. Yes, people who are spiritually and emotionally connected to the Eternal Creative Force discover their powerful potential as a creative personality and win the big prize in living. They become—yes, *you* become—a light in darkness. Light? Yes, an inspiration to your friends, neighbors, family, and community. You become a "light-turned-on person."

You become a cheerful light that replaces gloom with gladness. What a difference you make when your life becomes a light turned on! . . .

You become a guiding light. "If he could do it—maybe I can too." Your achievements become the creative inspirational light igniting the glow of hope in the drab, dark, dreary, discouraged minds of those who see your story lived out for all the world to read. The message you send is sincere and clear.

"I came from nowhere and went somewhere!" "I was a nobody—and I really became a somebody!" "I'm a bright light in a dark world!"

You can become that kind of inspiring person.

—◆—

Limited Resources

There are three sources of water in California: reservoirs, wells, and springs. In northern California there are times when the reservoirs are dry and empty. But these reservoirs are really not sources of water, just gathering places.

Is it possible that you may be backing away from great opportunities because you don't think you have what it takes to make it to the top, because you're not sure you have the inner resources (emotional, physical, and spiritual)? Is it because you just don't think you've got what it takes? Then you may be backing away from the challenge because your major source of nourishment is a *reservoir*. You're tapping your own human experiences and energy, and that has severe limitations! The truth is that you and I don't have what it takes to scale the peaks if we just depend on our own strength! If you depend on a reservoir to supply your resources, you'll run out of steam.

There's a second source of water in California, and that's the well. Wells are better than reservoirs because they tap the underground water table. But sometimes we have a problem in California because the water table has dropped so low that water no longer seeps into some of the wells and they run dry.

There are people who try to draw their energy and stamina for success not from the reservoir of their experience and knowledge but from the well of their inheritance—the family and tradition. The latter can be an enormous source of emotional nurture, but watch out: wells can run dry too!

Unlimited Resources

A third source of water is the mountain spring fed by the snow-capped glaciers that never thaw. *The spring flows from the snow-capped mountaintop!*

When you tap the spring of God's energetic flow, you have emotional power. That means power to feed enthusiasm, power to think positive thoughts, power to push negative thoughts out, power to maintain peace under enormous pressure.

You can have stamina unlimited! When you've tapped the spring, you don't trust your own strength! That's a reservoir! You can't just depend upon business associates, friends, or family. That's a well. You have the mountaintop spring! You are connected with Almighty God!

◆

Connect to Your Power Source

Listen to the call of your heart of hearts to become a believer in God. Your heart calls to your mind to listen to the spiritual impulses deep within yourself. Become a believer, and your heart will never allow your head to give up in frustration or failure. . . .

Will you—my reader friend—have the emotional energy that your goals demand from you? Yes—*if* you're connected to the eternal God who gave you the power of intuition along with the gift of intelligence.

The price must be paid. Connect with the God who gave you a head and a heart.

You're now in a holy and humble partnership with the Higher Power that mixed the genes into the one-of-a-kind person called *you*. Two priceless, precious gifts are yours: life and God's dream to be and become a bright light in a dark world.

Now trust Him; He'll speak to you from your heart of hearts, renewing you so that you'll never lack the emotional energy to keep on keeping on. He's promised again and again and again, "I will never leave you or forsake you."

◆

I Will Move . . .

Lord, I want your heart to be in my heart.
For in you I come alive, moving ahead
from boring death to exciting life!
In your promises, I will move from discouragement to hope.
In your pardon, I will move from shame to glory.
In your power, I will move from weakness to strength.
In your providence, I will move from failure to success!
Thank you, Lord.
Amen.

◆

Bars or Stars?

I know a woman who was "out" but became "in" when she learned to look at the bright side. She married a serviceman who took her away from her cultured, stimulating social scene in a big eastern city. He was assigned, of all places, to a California desert post. His duties and his salary kept them confined to the base. The military personnel bored her. The local community? In her words, "only hicks and Indians." In deep depression, she wrote her mother that she couldn't stand it any longer. She was leaving her husband. She was coming home. She was going back to the university.

Her mother wrote back: "Two people live in the same prison. One sees bars; the other stars. Don't leave, Honey. Bloom where you're planted."

She cried. That night she took a walk and saw the stars as she had never seen them in Philadelphia! She went to the library and picked up a book on stars. A new consuming interest was born! She stopped to talk history and culture with a local Indian woman. The woman not only taught her the native arts and crafts but embraced her as one of their own. She was "in" again!

—◇—

The Negatives Turn to Positives

Love yourself and you will find yourself loving the people around you. Love the people around you and you will find yourself loving God. Love God and you will find yourself conquering, with His help, the restrictive forces of negative thinking. Worry, resentment, fear, anxiety begin to leave you.

You face life with the confidence that "I can do all things through Christ who strengthens me." You attempt great things.

You are no longer bored. You are excited with the stimulation of a chance-taking project.

You are no longer lonely. You find yourself involved with people in the pursuit of a dream.

You no longer are beleaguered by an inferiority complex.

You are discovering that you can do more than you ever thought you could do.

You are no longer sad and forlorn. You are involved in the excitement of living. Teamed up with God, living in harmony with your neighbors, you are no longer a small person with feelings of inadequacy that shrink your soul; you are tall and great, facing life and the future courageously: "With God all things are possible." "If God is for me who can be against me?"

You no longer suffer from fatigue. You are energized by a dynamic enthusiasm as the power of love for yourself, love for others, and love for God surges through you.

You forget about your heartaches and your poor selfish griefs. No longer do you mournfully nurse your self-pity. You become a person with the power of God within you. Optimism, hopefulness, and cheerfulness become the dominant expressions of your life.

◈

The Positives Simply Soar

Each new positive accomplishment strengthens your sense of self-worth. You feel yourself growing taller and stronger.

You rise above your circumstances. You now have the courage to make decisions and to move forward confidently after you make these decisions

You discover that you are no longer trying to "impress people" with what an effective or successful person you are. You no longer are interested in "keeping up with the Joneses."

You no longer seek plaudits and applause—because you no longer need this external reassurance. You know that you and God are great friends. You have won God's approval. You learned to love yourself when you stood at the cross of Christ and heard the thunder of God's approval echoing from the mountain.

You discover that you are now genuinely humble. The false humility with which you dishonestly cloaked yourself was a phony impression-making maneuver. You drop it! Your hypocritical vanity is dissolved like the morning dew under the noonday sun.

You stand under the open sky beneath the love of God and simply know you are His child. Deep in your heart you know you are truly worthwhile.

You can even enjoy solitude without feeling lonely.

You discover that it's really true: when you learn to know and love yourself, you really come alive!

JUNE 7

———❖———

Old Dogs or New Creatures?

Can you change human nature? It depends on [whom] you choose to believe:

Freud would say, "No, you cannot change people." So he despaired of man. Shortly before he died, Sigmund Freud told Viktor Frankl, "The more I study man the more I despise him."

Marx would say, "Yes, change man's economic environment and you eliminate all human ill." So Freudians never make good Marxists.

Jesus Christ would say, "No, you cannot permanently change personality only through environment. Put a pear tree in an apple orchard and it's still a pear tree!" And he would also say, "Yes, you can change your life by changing your thinking. Allow the Holy Spirit to come into you and you'll be a new person." . . .

Alexander Pope prayed: "O God, make me a better man." His aide said, "It would be easier to make you a new man."

That is possible. St. Paul wrote, "If any one is in Christ he is a new creature." *How* does this happen? "Except you are born again you cannot enter the kingdom of heaven," Jesus said. Don't let the word "converted" scare you. Photosynthesis is the process by which the energy of sunlight is used to convert water or air into plant food. Life is converting food into energy; energy into action; mineral into vegetable, vegetable into animal; animal into human, and a selfish person . . . into a Christ-like believer. . . .

There are millions of human beings living on earth who have accepted Christ into their lives—and they've changed! They're able to love—unselfishly.

---◇---

The Hands of Jesus Christ

Dr. Louis Evans tells of visiting a mission station in Korea. A medical missionary friend invited him to witness a major operation. The surgical ward was a crude shop. The heat was stifling. The odors almost overwhelmed the visiting American minister. But the steady missionary doctor kept at his task with untiring skill. After seven hours he stood up, faced Dr. Evans, and announced that the job was done. They walked back to the modest office and Dr. Evans asked the missionary, "How much would you have been paid for that operation in America?" "Probably, five hundred dollars," the doctor answered. Evans said, "I'm curious. How much do you get here in Korea in this mission station?" The doctor picked from his desk a dented copper coin and said, "Well, to begin with—this. [The patient] came into our mission holding this coin and with tears in her eyes asked me, 'Doctor, do you suppose this would pay for an operation?' I looked at her and said, 'I think so!'" He went on, "To begin with—this dented coin, but most of all"—and tears filled his eyes—"most of all it makes me feel so good inside knowing that my hands for a few hours have been the hands of Jesus Christ healing a sick woman."

This is the answer.

This is the way.

It means that you, too, must come to Christ and invite Him to come into your life. If you do, He will fill you full. One of those who knew Him best tried it and left this triumphant testimony: "And of his fullness have we all received, grace for grace."

—◇—

Surrender to God's Power

When we love ourselves, we want to share ourselves. Only when we are self-assured, self-confident, and comfortable with ourselves do we dare to give ourselves to others. It takes great courage to love. For love means involvement, the risk of disappointment, the chance of exposing our intimate life to another person. Only the person who is really deeply self-trusting has the courage to love on this vulnerable level. How can we love ourselves deeply enough to risk sharing ourselves?

The only way I know for this kind of love, which is on the deepest level, to be able to enter and remain in a person's life is for the Spirit of Christ to come into one's life. When Christ's mind becomes a part of your mind, you begin to become a self-trusting, self-loving, self-sharing person. I offer a prayer that can lead you into a new life. Pray this prayer every day for thirty days.

Christ—here is my brain—think through it.
Christ—here is my face—glow through it.
Christ—here are my eyes—look at people through them.
Christ—here is my heart—love people with it.

To keep your self-love growing and glowing, follow a winner. Read His words. Meet Christ in the Bible. Join the happy Christians in your community church. You will catch His spirit. He will live His life through you. Your life can be a glove with Christ's hand in it. You'll find life is worth living when you find a God worth loving.

◈

I Want to Improve

O God, how thankful I am that you have come
into my life through the Holy Spirit.
I'm willing to say: "I'm not perfect, Lord!
I want to improve. Show me where I can."
So, Father, I sense that a miracle is
happening in my life right now.
You are doing something beautiful in
my heart this very moment.
I thank and praise you!
Amen.

—◇—

No Problem Is Permanent

Every mountain has a peak. Every valley has its low point. Life has its ups and downs, its peaks and its valleys. No one is up all the time, nor are they down all the time. Problems do end. They do go away. They are all resolved in time.

This principle is evident when you look carefully at history, for the history of humanity is a study in peaks and valleys. Humanity peaks at times when societies rise from decadence to a highly sophisticated state of civilization. Eventually, however, most cultures allow decay to set in. Rather than rooting out the negative influences, the human institutions adjust to the downward movement. The decline continues and accelerates until it reaches a low ebb, at which point it begins the long, slow ascent once more.

History teaches us that every problem has a life span. No problem is permanent. Do you have problems? They will pass; they will not last. Your problem will not live forever, but you will! Storms always give way to the sun. Winter always thaws into springtime. Your storm will pass. Your winter will thaw. Your problem will be resolved.

Lord, when I face a mountain, do not let me quit!
Give me the strength to keep on striving until I climb over,
find a pass through, or tunnel underneath.
And if my best efforts fail, give me the patience to stay
and the perception to see the possibilities
of turning my mountain into a gold mine with your help.
Amen.

Mountain-Moving Faith

"If you have faith as a grain of mustard seed you can say to this mountain: move! And it will move! And nothing will be impossible to you!"

There are many people who claim to live by faith but remain low achievers. We all know individuals who claim to exercise real faith yet they accomplish little or nothing. What's wrong? Frequently failure is the result of a too-shallow faith.

I walk to the beach and I see people cautiously putting their toes in the edge of the ocean. They splash around ankle-deep, come back to lie down in the sun, and go home claiming they have been swimming.

There are others who wade waist-deep in the water before they turn back to lie on the warm sand.

Then there is the real venturer who moves steadily deeper until the water reaches his shoulders and he begins to swim. He has moved to the deeper level and can honestly claim that he has been swimming. Mountain-moving faith is not merely touching your toes in the water. Mountain-moving faith is faith that dares to step into deep water.

———◇———

Start with a Dream

Mountain-moving faith begins with a dream. Unquestionably the greatest power in the world is the power of a creative idea. All success begins with a dream. One of America's great teachers was Thomas S. Kelly. The secret of his effective life, according to Rufus Jones, goes back to a single moment in Kelly's freshman year at college when he had a dream—and he said, "I'm going to make my life a miracle!" Someone said, "There are no great men: only great ideas." Indeed, you can often measure the size of a person by the size of his dreams.

Faith begins with an act of imagining. If you don't have a dream, how can dreams come true? Begin now by using this God power within yourself to paint a picture of what you would like to accomplish.

Reject all impossibility thoughts, all "handicap concepts," and all disadvantage complexes. Imagine yourself as a friend of the mighty, a partner of the wealthy, and a co-worker with God. Faith begins with a dream.

Cultivate Desire

Faith in deeper water is wanting something so badly that some-day, somehow, somewhere, sometime, you know you shall have it. More faith is shattered by lack of desire than by real doubt.

No one will ever believe that he can move a mountain unless he really wants that mountain to move. Almost anything can be accomplished by the person who really wants to succeed. The old adage is so true: if there's a will, there's a way.

We believe what we want to believe!

Believing is wanting!

Apply this definition of faith to your project and your dreams. To begin with, you must know what you want. Not a few people fail because they have neglected to visualize in detail what they were trying to achieve. If you have a confused and muddled picture of what you are going after, do not be surprised if you fail. Therefore, an early step in mountain-moving faith is forming a detailed mental picture of your dream.

As the sharp details of your dream come into clear mental focus, you will find your enthusiasm mounting to an ever higher pitch.

If you want your dream badly enough, you will plan, organize, reorganize, and work, until you get what you want. Great desire marshals great determination. And success awaits the person who believes in "never say never." You never really fail until you stop wanting. Faith is wanting something with all your heart!

—◇—

Take a Risk

Doubt is frequently a lack of courage. Fear of embarrassment, along with fear of involvement, or fear of personal self-sacrifice, is enough to keep many a person from wanting to make a commitment of faith to an idea, a dream, a project, or a cause. With God on your side you will dare to run risks!

Mountain-moving faith is not merely dreaming and desiring; it is daring to risk failure. For faith is making a decision with no guarantee of success. If success is certain, then a venture is no longer an act of faith. Faith without risk is a contradiction. Faith is taking a chance on something before you can be sure how everything will finally work out. Remember: Every time you make a choice you take a chance.

Even indecision is a decision. And even if you decide to do nothing you run the risk of failing to attempt what might have become a marvelous miracle. Don't forget: "The saddest words of tongue or pen are these—it might have been."

Dare to Risk Disappointment

Many people fail and never know it. They go through life without a single apparent setback. They never suffer embarrassment or reversals. They think they are successful. But the truth is, they fail because they neglected to spot and develop the once-in-a-lifetime opportunity. They are failures but do not know it.

Faith is daring to risk disappointment. Possibility Thinkers have cast the fear of personal disappointment from their thinking! How many people never enter a contest, never compete in the games, never commit their lives to something that has the prospect of greatness, for fear of losing?

"If you never try, you will never lose." How my heart sank when I heard that depressing and erroneous statement by an otherwise intelligent young man. "It just is not true. You can lose what you could have had," I told him.

One of the tragedies of life is that too many people deliberately set their goals too low, to reduce the possibility of disappointment. Obviously, our goals must be realistic, but high enough so that success can be termed a miracle. Not a few people claim to be a success because they've reached every goal in life. The truth is, they are really failures because their goals were deceptively low.

On the other hand, many people have been proclaimed failures because they never achieved their highest goal, simply because their goal was too high. They did not reach their goal, but they did reach their maximum potential. And that's being a success! Success is not necessarily reaching your goal, but success is reaching your maximum possibility in the light of the opportunities that came your way.

A Daring Faith

Faith is daring to risk public criticism. The truth is that every pioneer project is criticized by negative people. Now, public opinion is not to be totally disregarded, but it must be put in its proper place. We should remember that we must live with some people part of our life; we must live with a few people most of our life; but we must live with ourselves all of our life; and we must live with God forever! Ask these decision-making questions in this order: (1) What does God think? (2) What do you, in your own heart, think? (3) What do your wise friends think? (4) What would the public think? Public opinion is the last question to be asked—not the first! . . .

Faith is daring to risk imperfection. "If it can't be a best-seller, I won't publish it," I once thought. Until this idea struck me: *better to do something imperfectly than to do nothing perfectly!*

The tragic truth is that much of our efforts would be overwhelmingly successful if we dared to run the risk of mediocrity. What we judge to be mediocre may be judged by others to be excellent. Norman Vincent Peale worked long and hard on his first manuscript. Finally, convinced in his own mind that it was not good enough, he threw it in a wastebasket. Fortunately, it was picked out of the basket, sent to the publishers, and appeared in the bookstores of the country under the title *A Guide to Confident Living*. It has sold more than a million copies.

Faith is daring to be a chance-taker. Do you know what Possibility Thinkers fear more than failure? It is the fear of becoming stale, stagnant, and tired. It is the fear of the adventure-stifling, courage-strangulating inclination to "play it safe."

$\diamond$

Self-Confidence Equals Security

What is the spirit of security but a deep belief in yourself? What is insecurity but a lack of faith in one's own ability?

How do you give people a sense of security? By giving them a chance to build faith in themselves! Self-reliance and self-confidence are real security. When Communism collects people together and spares them from competition, protects them from the possibility of failure, and shelters them from the possibility of poverty, is it really offering security? It is perhaps eliminating the fear of poverty and starvation, but *the absence of fear is no proof of courage.*

Play-it-safe people may not be afraid. But this does not mean that they are brave. What would happen if they had to face danger? Suddenly they would discover that they lacked real courage. Communism offers a counterfeit security, for real security is self-confidence.

The priceless gift of self-confidence can only be acquired when you succeed after being exposed to possible failure. Exposure to risk is the only route to real self-confidence. Self-confidence cannot be inherited. It must be earned by each individual, each generation, each new regime. And the only way to earn it is by taking a noble risk, an honorable chance, a glorified gamble. Self-confidence cannot be taught; it must be caught! And risk-running, chance-taking, is the only way to catch it. Mountain-moving faith succeeds in building self-confidence through chance-taking. Without self-confidence, faith will never muster and demonstrate mountain-moving power.

——◇——

Get Started

It is not enough to dream, desire, and dare. Mountain-moving faith now begins to act as if nothing is going to stop the dream from succeeding. We all know people who think great ideas and dream daring dreams, but never get started. Probably because as long as they postpone beginning, these big pretenders are still playing it safe.

Faith must move from the level of imagination into the level of conversation and then into the level of concrete organization. Get started! Do something!

It is my observation that real support for a cause never comes until we begin to exercise an aggressive faith.

God seldom performs a miracle until we try. And great faith involves going out on a limb where we run the risk of failure, possible embarrassment, and potential defeat. God does not allow us to face humiliating personal disaster if we have carefully and prayerfully ventured forth in a practical, human-need-filling, inspiring, exceptional faith-project! Someone said: "Even a turtle doesn't get ahead unless he sticks his neck out."

Although we don't like to give up control, sometimes it's the way God really reveals Himself. When we have to "let go and let God," miracles happen!

—◇—

Get Moving

One of the most helpful sentences I ever heard was from the lips of Professor Milton Hinga, a history professor at Hope College, Holland, Michigan. When he found out that none of the members of his history class had even started their term papers, he rose, paced the room, and said, "I am about to tell you the most important thing you will ever hear!"

Every eye focused upon him, waiting breathlessly for his great pronouncement. He spoke softly but firmly: "I don't care if you flunk. I don't care if you forget everything that I ever teach you in this class. But I never want you to forget this next sentence." After a dramatic pause he shouted out: "Beginning is half done!"

Do you have a good idea? Have you discussed it with knowledgeable people? And are you convinced that it is practical, inspiring, and exceptional? Do you dare to run the risks involved? Then get started today.

Too busy? Then maybe it is time to hire or ask somebody to help you.

This is often the beginning point. If you have a good idea, if it has passed the test of wise people, then it may pay you to hire the person who can get the project successfully off the ground. It may even pay to borrow the money to hire people to successfully launch your venture. This may be the starting point for you.

Whatever you do—get started. Beginning is half done.

Fence-sitting faith doesn't even have the strength to move a molehill. We can't expect God to move a mountain if we are not interested enough to get started.

JUNE 21

———◇———

Expect Success

Not a few people think, talk, and actually begin, only to fail because their faith has not been deep enough to reach the deep expecting level of belief. They had enough faith to use their imagination. They had enough faith to enter into intelligent conversation with knowledgeable people. They had enough faith to actually establish an organization and begin their project. They had imagination, conversation, organization, but they lacked anticipation. After they got their venture launched, they began to worry, wonder, and doubt whether they would really ever succeed.

Dr. Norman Vincent Peale said, "Hope is the great power that can move you to success. Why? Because when a man expects to win, he does not hold anything back, but gives his project all that he's got. Most people fail not because they lack ability, intelligence, or opportunity, but they fail because they don't give it all they've got."

When you expect success, then you hold nothing back, but sink your last dime, spend your second-wind energy, and gamble your priceless reputation, confident that you'll make it. Such extreme dedication almost always leads to success, for when people know that you have given your wonderful idea all that you've got, they will march to your side and help you on to victory and success. One of the world's greatest religious statesmen moved mountains with this statement: "Attempt great things for God and expect great things from God."

—◆—

Don't Get Discouraged

Do not be discouraged if you do not accomplish everything that you set out to accomplish.

Surely if you do not expect to succeed you will hold back your full power, investment, and enthusiasm. Immediately the kind of people who could help to move you on to victory begin to draw back. Your conservative and cautious attitude will reflect itself in an anxious look on your face that will disturb and discourage people from helping you.

There are two major reasons why people fail. Both stem from a lack of mountain-moving faith. (1) People who fail are often people who are indecisive. They cannot make decisions swiftly and surely. The fast-moving opportunity is past before they decide— too late—to take hold. (2) Then some decisive people fail because, after making the decision, they fail to move forward with an expectant confidence. They grab the opportunity, only to lose nerve, get cold feet, and begin to wonder if they have done the right thing. They have gripped the plow but now they are looking back. Want to be a success? Develop the ability to appraise opportunities intelligently, seize opportunities swiftly, and promote these opportunities confidently.

———◇———

Affirming Faith

Faith is affirming success before it comes. Faith is making claims to victory before it is achieved. This is very difficult to do, but most important.

Our instinctive sense of modesty and honesty tends to restrain us from making public statements of our anticipated success. We sense that any announcement of success before it is within our grasp is a sin of presumption and proud boasting. So we have a natural compulsion to say nothing, keep quiet, hope for the best, and when we have won we will make our joyous announcement.

Was St. Paul modest when he said, "I can do all things through Christ who strengthens me"? Was he exaggerating a bit? Was he literally truthful in this affirmation? Or was this an extreme exercise of mountain-moving faith talking?

The truth is that mountain-movers are people who boldly predict success. They know that nothing succeeds like success. They know that no one likes to follow a loser. They know they have to convey an image of winning or they will never gain the following they need to achieve their goal. So their bold prediction, their brash announcement, is not immodesty—nor is it dishonesty—nor is it cocky pride—it is *faith in depth!*

—◇—

Great Affirmations

Affirming—this is enthusiasm-generating faith. Great affirmations heighten the sense of expectancy and generate great enthusiasm.

Affirm success and you will visualize yourself winning. When you imagine yourself winning then that mysterious force of enthusiasm suddenly surges through your being.

Because enthusiastic people are happy people, they are energetic and ambitious people.

So enthusiastic people are spirit-lifting, morale-boosting, talent-attracting, hope-generating people.

It's no wonder that affirmative people magnetically attract to themselves gifted people who generously offer their talent, time, or treasure to make the exciting dream come true.

"Tell people confidently that you are going to win," I advised a young man running for office. "But what if I lose? What would I say then?" My answer was swift: "If you lose you can walk right up to them and say, 'Well, at least I had the faith that I was going to win!' Have you ever seen anyone win public office when he did not predict victory?"

It's a cinch—few men can move mountains all by themselves. And you will never attract or inspire people to help you unless you can offer them strong hope of ultimate success.

Is your faith deep enough to predict success before it is within your grasp?

———◇———

Waiting Power

The kind of faith that moves mountains is a faith that has great waiting power.

You have left the shallows, the water has gone over your head, you have taken the great plunge, you can no longer feel bottom beneath your feet, but you have not yet started to swim. This is the sweating phase of faith.

In every development there is a stage where you've thought it, started it, expected it, and affirmed it. Now you've passed the point of no return but cannot yet understand how ultimate success will be yours. Great and unexpected problems assault you. But you cannot back down, you cannot run away, you can only keep going and hope for the best.

Waiting—this is faith in deep waters. Almost every venture goes through a period of time when problems are overwhelming. This is the time to remind yourself that mountain-moving faith is faith with hold-the-line power.

How often I have been asked by discouraged people, "Reverend, I have prayed, but it doesn't seem to work for me. I have tried to believe in God, but it doesn't seem to help me. What's wrong with my faith?" In almost every instance I have to advise them that there is one vital ingredient missing in their faith. And that dynamic ingredient is patience.

Faith is *patience!* People who really succeed are people who know that every project goes through phases when there is nothing to do but wait. The danger is that we may be tempted in this dreary time to quit.

———◇———

Accept or Surrender

We all face situations when our mountain does not budge, in spite of all we do.

Then, it seems to me, the only thing we can do is offer that profound prayer of faith first offered by Jesus Christ. When death by crucifixion seemed imminent, He offered this faith-packed prayer: "My Father, all things are possible unto Thee. Nevertheless, not my will, but Thine be done." "Thy will be done" towers above all human utterances as the supreme statement of faith on the deepest level!

Mountain-moving faith is surrendering—letting go and letting God take over. "Thy will be done" is unquestionably the ultimate declaration of faith that can possibly fall from the lips of a human being. . . .

Recently a handsome young husband lost his wife. We failed in our efforts to help him overcome the mountain of grief that cast a black shadow of despair over his soul. Then came the day of the funeral. I prayed silently for him. After everyone had left the chapel, the grief-stricken husband and I stood alone at the casket. Then the miracle happened. Looking up with tearful face, he prayed, "Lord, I give her back to you." His faith reached mountainous heights. He stood tall and straight again! As he regained an amazing composure he looked at me and said, "She's in good hands now." And he walked forthrightly and strongly away. He had surrendered her to God. In surrendering, his faith found the power to move the mountain of grief. And the sunshine of warm peace fell into his mind.

———◇———

Only Time Will Tell

The longer I study human life the more I realize that only God knows what's good and what's bad for us. One of my favorite stories is the classic story of the Chinese who had one horse and one son. One day his horse broke out of the corral and fled to the freedom of the hills. The neighbors came around that night and chattered, "Your horse got out? What bad luck!" "Why," the old Chinese said, "how do you know it's bad luck?" Sure enough, the next night the horse came back to his familiar corral for his usual feeding and watering, leading twelve wild stallions with him! The farmer's son saw the thirteen horses in the corral, slipped out, and locked the gate. Suddenly [the man] had thirteen horses instead of none. The neighbors heard the good news and came chattering to the farmer, "Oh, you have thirteen horses! What good luck!" And the old Chinese answered, "How do you know that's good luck?"

Some days later his strong young son was trying to break one of the wild stallions only to be thrown off and break a leg. The neighbors came back that night and passed another hasty judgment: "Your son broke his leg? What bad luck!" And the wise father answered again, "How do you know it's bad luck?" Sure enough, a few days later a Chinese warlord came through town and conscripted every able-bodied young man, taking them off to war, never to return again. But the young man was saved because of his broken leg. Only God knows what's good for us and what's bad for us.

"All things work together for good to those who love God." When we learn this lesson, then it becomes possible for us to pray the surrendering prayer of deepest faith, "Thy will be done."

———◇———

Exercising Faith

The core of Possibility Thinking is the mental activity we call "positive assuming." Even though the idea may have been unsuccessfully tried before, you should do the following:

- Assume that the times may have changed.

- Assume that nothing is as powerful as an idea whose time has come.

- Assume that there are solutions to the problems that have defeated the dream before.

- Assume that there are solutions to the money problems.

- Assume that costs can be cut, revenue can be increased, or the project can be refinanced over a longer period of time.

- Assume that smarter people can be either hired or invited as partners to make this challenging idea possible.

- Assume that obstructionists can be bypassed, isolated, or invited to join as partners in prosperity in a new joint venture.

- Assume that instead of a collision you could form a coalition!

Now you're exercising what religious people call *faith*. Faith is sometimes spelled A-S-S-U-M-E.

Mountains Melt

A lack of self-confidence is one of the four most common failure-producing factors that must be overcome if you hope to become the person you want to be. Believe me, mountains melt before the self-reliant, self-confident person.

Henry Ford said, "Think you can, think you can't; either way you'll be right." Be careful of what you imagine yourself becoming. There is an abundance of scientific evidence that an individual's mental picture of himself, more than any other factor, sets the ultimate boundaries of his achievements. We now know that the human brain, like an intricate automatic guidance system, will steer your life toward a realization of the mental self-image you feed into it. Your subconscious will work for you or against you. You make the determination by the self-fulfilling dreams or the self-defeating limitations you feed into it. When this law is understood and applied, we see revolutionary changes in human personality. Deeply ingrained habits, fundamental behavior patterns, even talents and abilities, have been miraculously altered by persons who have believed, acted upon, and used this law of self-image psychology.

—◇—

Qualities of the
Self-Confident Winner

Imagination: Self-confident people imagine themselves being the people they want to become. They ignore the way they are now.

Commitment: So strong is the desire to achieve their dream that self-confident people totally commit themselves to their goal. It is an unconditional, nonnegotiable commitment. The power of a totally committed person is incalculable.

Affirmation: First imagine. Then commit. Now affirm that you are going to succeed. Verbalize your positive thinking. This will exercise and vitalize your self-confidence. At the same time, you will cause others to believe in your eventual success. Now a wonderful thing happens. As other people begin to believe in you they will want to help, which adds fresh propellant to your rocketing self-confidence!

Never Give Up: Never, never, never give up! Patience and persistence are the crowning qualities of self-confident champions. Defeat and failure are heretical concepts that cannot and will not be contemplated.

The initials of these four qualities spell I C-A-N! That's self-confidence! Properly directed and constructively channeled, self-confidence becomes the very power of Almighty God surging, throbbing, pulsating, vibrating with the force of spiritual electricity through the human personality, transforming a listless, lifeless, apathetic person into an inspired, inflamed dynamo who catapults his life to greatness!

Build Your Self-Confidence

If you assume that you are inferior, you will suffer a disastrous failure. If you assume problems will block and defeat you, that if you try you'll only get hurt again, you have already fashioned another oppressive concept in your mind: "I can't do it! It won't work for me." . . .

Break this binding chain with powerful, God-filled affirmations:

- "If God be for me who can be against me?"
- "I can do all things through Christ who strengthens me."
- "All things are possible to me if I will believe."

I broke the chain of inferiority feelings within myself and acquired self-confidence through two Bible verses.

- "Be confident in this one thing, that God who has begun a good work in you (He has been giving you the will, the hope, the dream, the desire) will complete it!" (Phil. 1:6). (He will give you the secret, the strength, and the skill to succeed!)
- "For it is God working in you, giving you the will and the power to achieve His purposes" (Phil. 2:13).

Memorize and saturate your thinking with these Bible verses.

—◇—

Nature or Nurture?

Is creativity a gift or is it an art? Is it an inherited talent that you have—or don't have? Or is it a skillful way of thinking that can be artfully learned by any person? There is abundant and mounting evidence that the latter is the truth.

Dr. Edwin H. Land, inventor of the Polaroid camera, has experimented with this phenomenon of creativity. He has placed blue-collar workers alongside practicing, creative people, active in research. "It's amazing—the blue-collar people are all becoming creative," he reports!

Among those trillions of cells in your brain, there lie thousands of brilliant but slumbering cells that are charged with vast powers waiting to be aroused, harnessed, and unleashed. If you can discover a way to stimulate them, you'll be amazed at your own brilliance and intelligence.

—◆—

The Gift of Imagination

Claim this remarkable, miraculous gift and you will be able to see a thing before it is. Why, this is a divine quality! It may well be the most impressive evidence of the reality of God coming to live and flow constructively and creatively through human beings! This could be the proof of the biblical teaching that "Man is created in the *image* of God."

"Imageofgodinus" is the way I write the word "imagination"! Yes, imagination is the "image-of-God-in-us"! Like a window, it can sparkle clear and clean, allowing a clear vision to the horizon. Or it can be covered with a film, thin at first; then slowly, imperceptibly, a thickening layer of sediment accumulates on the defenseless glass until the sparkling mirror quality of this window of the soul, where God shines through, is darkened and dulled, distorting the picture. Fatigue, frustration, failures, and fears soil this screen where God wants to project a clear readout of his programming for our lives!

So revitalize your imagination! And a darkened mind will light up in Technicolor! Action! Sound! Energy! Enthusiasm! Drive! Determination! Zeal! Zest! Vitality!

A Clear Vision

Look what happens to the person whose imagination is revitalized! The window is washed. The screen is cleared, the projection
sharply focused. Suddenly fears are wiped out. The darkness is
washed away. The brightly glowing vision appears on the mind's
inner screen. An inexplicable surge of overpowering determination to strive and succeed energizes the taproot of human motivation. You are hooked on a happy goal! Nobody can stop you now.
You see the vision clearly. You catch an unmistakable picture of
the dream that God sketched for your life. You're a dancing
teenager again. You're a budding Olympic contender. You're an
up-and-coming achiever. "Watch out, world, here I come."

Imagination, what an amazing channel of immeasurable spiritual power! Imagination—it's the audio and visual channel that
God uses to communicate His dreams to your consuming consciousness. Wow! When your imagination is turned on, you are *really alive.* No chemical or drug can produce a high comparable to
this healthy, holy high. But turn off this imagination and allow
the screen to become dark and you are suddenly bored, dull, and
boring—and terribly vulnerable to an unholy host of potentially
destructive stimuli that seek to fill your inner emotional vacuum
and satisfy your heart's craving for excitement.

Revitalize Your Imagination

How do we revitalize imagination? There are many ways. Study the timeless wisdom found in the Bible. Read inspiring stories in magazines and on the sports and business pages of the newspaper. Observe and experience what is around you, and you will see countless living illustrations of great and wonderful achievements being racked up by people just like you! Let their accomplishments inspire your imagination. . . .

How do you revitalize your imagination? I asked this question of a friend who is extremely creative. His answer was, "My imagination is rekindled and renewed when I relate to people who really respect me and build me up." So you revitalize your imagination by revitalizing your relationships. Draw close to Possibility Thinking persons who see the potential within you and honestly affirm your value and worth. As you receive and respect their affirming compliments, you'll begin to believe in yourself too!

So begin by revitalizing your relationship with the one person who always builds you up and never puts you down. His name is Jesus Christ. Pray. Simply close your eyes. Talk to Him. Be quiet and give Him a chance to speak to you. Ask Him simple and sincere questions. Sit quietly and wait for His answers. Give Him a chance to draw a picture in your imagination of the wonderful, holy, positive things He'd like you to do and be. Embrace His vision! Relish this divine delicacy of inspired and sanctified imagination. Feast on this inspiration from God that can and will become reality. Christ's power is actually evident in your life through imagination! There's no telling how far you will go now!

The Power of the
Sanctified Imagination

It's easy to understand how the imagination operates. When you draw a clear mental picture and get a sharp mental definition of what you really want, then you become enthusiastic about it. Enthusiasm produces ambition. And with the fresh spurt of ambition you begin to pray, plan, and plug; and before you know it your project is off the ground.

What is the secret power of the Possibility Thinkers? It is their faith. And what is this faith? It is the power of God working through their God-sparked imagination.

Harness the sacramental power of a sanctified imagination.

Truly a sanctified imagination has sacramental power. Religion defines sacrament as a sacred channel through which God performs His great miracles. Let God do something *now*—Let Him spark His great ideas into your imaginating mind! Unchain your imagination. Let this God-given power within you go free!

188

Imagine Being a Success with People

To succeed in the field of human relations, polish your own personality with your imagination. Visualize yourself as a relaxed, charming, confident, poised, smiling person. Firmly hold this mental image of yourself and you will become this kind of person. . . . This is the exciting truth: your imagination has the power to transform and recreate your personality.

More exciting news! You can actually change the personalities of other people through the power of your own imagination. I sat in on a board of directors meeting recently. When I entered the room, I was greeted by the cold, unfriendly stares of six men. Personalities, like feelings, are terribly contagious. . . . Then a wonderful thing happened. A strong, friendly personality entered the room. He radiated warmth as his face beamed steadily. His infectious smile refused to fade before the icy stares of these important men. To my amazement within five minutes the personalities of the other people in the room were transformed. Soon we were talking and joking and sincerely enjoying each other's company. After the meeting, I asked my friend how he managed to change these stuffed shirts into wonderful people. His secret was simple. "I paused before I entered that room and imagined myself as a strong, dominant, friendly, down-to-earth person. I imagined the men on the other side of the door as good fellows. I visualized them returning my smiles, and reflecting the kindness I was radiating toward them." This man had discovered how to use his imagination to change the personalities of people.

Imagine Meeting New People

Do you have a problem meeting people? Is it hard for you to make new friends and acquaintances? Then use, with great success, the power of your imagination. I discovered this technique in starting our church. Because I had no members, I decided to go down the street and ring doorbells, telling my story to people face-to-face. Frankly, I trembled at the thought of going from door to door, meeting all these new people. I imagined being rudely rebuffed every time I rang a doorbell. Generally, we get what we expect. I would walk timidly up to the front door, secretly hoping no one would be at home. More than once I left without ringing the bell. I simply got "cold feet" and went back to my car. Suddenly, in answer to my prayer for divine help and guidance, God sparked my imagination. I began to visualize warm, wonderful people on the other side of the doors—people who were eager to meet a new minister. That did it! I approached every door thereafter with this belief: "Behind that door is someone who is going to become a lifelong friend of mine. I am about to make the acquaintance of someone who will become one of my most loyal friends." Try this technique with problem people. Imagine them as really fine people at heart. Believe that's what they might become.

—◇—

Imagine the Person
You Were Meant to Be

As you face life, throw your shoulders back, look into the sun, and thank God you're a human being! When God made you, He gave you what was given to no other living organism in the universe— the immeasurable power to visualize great dreams! This stupendous truth has never been more forcefully, exquisitely phrased than in these inspiring lines: "What is man that you are mindful of him and the son of man that you visit him, for you have made him a little lower than God" (Ps. 8:4–5). The daring creativity of human imagination is exciting proof that you are made in the image of God. What an imagination God has displayed! His infinite mind visualized a universe so grandiose in scale, so immense in distance, that no human being will ever be able to see it all in a single lifetime.

Now, the exciting news is that the Creator of Life has shared with the human race His creative power of imagination.

This imagination is latent in your mind this very moment—and it has the power to make you. "As a man thinks in his heart so is he."

Imagine Being What You Really Want to Be

Use your God-sparked imagination to gain self-confidence. Imagine yourself as inferior, inadequate, mediocre, and that's all you will ever be. Imagine yourself as top notch, successful, a person who is getting ahead, and you will move forward.

I recently heard about William E. Constable, who worked in a lime quarry in Indiana for nine years. One day he came to the conclusion that "my life was a waste, so I decided to get busy and do something with it." That night he came home from the quarry and announced to his wife that he was going to become a lawyer. He resumed his education and finally enrolled in Indiana University. He continued to work in the quarry eight hours a day while he went to school. "My wife and three kids really helped," he added gratefully. He graduated from Indiana University in 1966 and guess what. He was elected to Phi Beta Kappa! His grade average was 3.95 out of a possible four points. He has gone on to law school. How did he do it? How did he work eight hours a day and come out on top of his college class? Besides crediting the company that employed him and praising his family's cooperation, he offered this insight: "You can do a lot of studying in thirty minutes if you have to." To sum it up, there came that moment when he imagined himself being an attorney and said, "Just because I've spent nine years in a quarry is no reason I can't be a lawyer."

Imagine Changing
Your Appearance

Imagination can transform your physical appearance. Imagine yourself with twinkling eyes, a beaming face, a radiant personality; hold that picture in your mind and you will become that kind of person. Think of yourself as ugly, unattractive, and your eyes will take on a dullness, your facial muscles will droop, and a gloomy appearance will suddenly make you unattractive indeed.

Beauty is mind-deep. You are as pretty—or as unattractive—as you think you are. Visualize yourself as a pleasant, friendly, cheerful, laughing, sparkling person and your imagination will make you into that kind of person. Now exercise this positive imagination daily and the "smile muscles" will become so strong that your facial appearance will actually be transformed. Through the power of imagination I actually trimmed forty pounds of unsightly fat from my body. I drew a mental image of the kind of physique I wanted and held that vision before me constantly. I also directed the negative power of my imagination toward positive ends in this way: when I saw a luscious piece of banana cream pie, I pictured in my mind a vision of a fat, sloppy, undisciplined man. It's amazing how your imagination can affect the appeal of food! Focus clearly on the screen of your mind the image of the kind of person you want to be and let your God-sparked imagination work its miracles.

You Can Begin with Nothing

Dreams cost nothing. Do you have a dream? Are you facing money problems? Remember this: all great projects begin with a dream. Projects can be started without a single cent!

The most valuable things in life are free. An idea, an hour in the early morning, a friend who encourages, the freedom to sell your idea, an article in the newspaper. All of these are free! So is talk. If you have a need-filling, God-glorifying, humanity-inspiring, imaginative idea, share it with trusting Possibility Thinkers and you will at least give the dream a chance to come alive. Truly, the most valuable product in the world is an idea. Good ideas magnetically attract support from unexpected sources.

—◇—

The Impossible Idea

To whom can God entrust His dream? The wrong person would laugh it off or ridicule the impossible dream, rejecting it out of hand in sarcastic scorn. God must be careful where He drops the seed lest it fall on hard ground—a mind infected with cynicism. Or it might fall on shallow ground, where it could sprout but later die for lack of deep soil, in want of nourishment. God must avoid the mind that would welcome with instant enthusiasm the infant dream, only to abandon it in times of stress.

God must find the right mind to which He can send this impossible idea! Someone who will receive it, respect it, reverence it, feed it, protect it, nourish it, mother it to maturity, and then reproduce it! Yes—reproduce it—for no dream is ever *a* dream! Many apples will grow from one seed that is planted, nurtured, and nourished. So God looks for someone who won't ignore or abort it simply because "It's impossible." The Almighty looks for a Possibility Thinker. Somewhere on planet earth some simple, ordinary person who gets a bright idea "out of the blue"! God has made His move. Contact has been made between heaven and earth. The divine creative process has asserted itself once more. Creation is eternal—like success, an unending process!

The same wonderful spirit that moved in the beginning of creation, bringing life onto a dead planet, brings life into otherwise dead spirits with the spark of a high and honorable vision of fabulous possibilities!

—◇—

Believe in the Dream

Success begins once we start to believe in the beautiful dream that God sends us. How marvelous that our response was positive and not negative. How remarkable that the simple dream was not dismissed offhandedly as an impossibility, when in fact the moment was a meeting of a human mind with the dream of the Creator—God!

Once success starts it can never stop. For success is never-ending. Even the setting of the sun does not mark an end to the day that is past, for that day is given eternal life as it becomes a part of irrevocable history!

How far will the dream travel? How long will its life span be? Will the new life that stirs in the womb go to full term and be born to live out a normal life span? Or will it be aborted intentionally or by accident or injury and labeled a miscarriage? Even so, it will be remembered. Positive ideas have instant immortality, even if they die in the womb. They have left their imprint in the memory. More often than not, the idea will be reborn, renewed! And if it amounts to nothing more than a temporary recollection, it will make a new impact on the human consciousness. So it isn't totally dead after all. It is really true—success is never-ending and failure is never final!

Blessed are those whose dreams are shaped by their hopes, not by their hurts.

—◇—

My Walk

O God, I'm inspired.
For you have just impressed
this truth into my mind:
The most powerful force in the world
is a positive idea in the mind of a
believer who is walking in your will!
I now reach forth my life and say,
"God, put my life into the center of your will."
Amen.

—◇—

Dream Large

If you can achieve the dream without the help of God, then it is too small. Make your dreams big enough for God to fit in, for God's dreams are always so large that they require His help to make them come true. This is God's built-in defense system to keep us humble. Then when the success is realized, we'll not forget who really gets the credit!

The Dream of Doing leads to success. The Dream of Being leads to significance.

———◆———

Unexpected Opportunities

When possibility thinkers are surprised by a spontaneous and un-expected opportunity, they don't irresponsibly seize it. Nor do they (with equal irresponsibility) allow the suggestion to be dismissed, offhand and outright, with a careless, cavalier negative response. Instead, they treat the fresh possibility with reverent respect: "I'll take a new look at my schedule. Perhaps I'll need to realign my priorities."

Of course, there will be risks. Every decision commands a price—known or unknown. But you can't *escape* all risks by *avoiding* all risks. Remember, before you turn your back on the new possibility, that you risk losing what you might have won. . . .

The Quakers were taught to pray each night before they went to sleep. They were also taught to pray on awakening each morn-ing, seeking divine wisdom by drawing up a fresh list of what they could do that day. The new day might be a virtual repeat of the day before, but not necessarily! The morning news comes on. An unexpected telephone call interrupts the day's plans. Or a con-versation you had with someone changes priorities with a new idea!

Providence often challenges our careful planning with an un-invited and unexpected fresh possibility! So make out your new priority list every morning. You'll be surprised at how frequently your priorities can and should be urgently, wisely, even compas-sionately revised.

Waste Not, Want Not

Every idea is worth considering. Most ideas are worthy of action. The most tragic waste is the waste of a good idea. I ask you now: Is there some great idea in your life that you have still not dealt with affirmatively?

Everyone has within him some idea of something that he should have started but hasn't. Maybe it's to quit smoking. Maybe it's to lose weight. Maybe it's to get started on a physical fitness program. Maybe it's to join a church. Maybe it's to accept Jesus Christ as your Savior and Lord. Maybe it's to read the Bible, which you may never have done. Maybe it's to start a new business. Maybe it's to go back to school. Maybe it's to take a positive attitude toward your marriage, discarding the negative attitude you've had far too long. Maybe it's to quit drinking. I don't know what it is, but everyone, I have no doubt, has an idea of some area in which he should be taking some action for self-improvement.

Now—what will you do with that idea? America is known for its waste. We waste money, energy, gasoline, fuel, time, clothing, and paper. But nothing is as tragic as the waste of a good idea! So, if there's a good idea in your mind right now, don't waste it!

Thank you, Lord, for the exciting ideas you are waiting to send into my thinking mind! I'd explode with enthusiasm if I could think of all the positive thoughts waiting to come out of my God-inspired brain. Amen.

———◈———

TLC for Your Ideas

Beginning is half done! Get started! Winning starts with beginning!

What kind of a person are you? Often we hear the question: How do you treat people? A far more important question is this: How do you treat ideas?

Treat ideas like newborn babies:

Treat them tenderly . . .
  They can die pretty quickly.
Treat them gently . . .
  They can be bruised in infancy.
Treat them respectfully . . .
  They could be the most valuable things
  that ever come into your life.
Treat them protectively . . .
  Don't let them get away.
Treat them nutritionally . . .
  Feed them, and feed them well.
Treat them antiseptically . . .
  Don't let them get infected with the germs
  of negative thoughts.
Treat them responsibly!
  Respond! Act! Do something with them!

Within You, Waiting

A man from the Orient once traveled around the world in search of the wisest guru. He was told that this man lived in a cave high up in the Himalayas. So he loaded his horse with supplies, set off across mountains and deserts, and after months of traveling, came to the foot of a high mountain. He led his horse up the narrow path through the crevices until he came to a cave.

"Are you the guru who is known around the world for his wisdom?" he asked the old man sitting in the cave.

The old man rose to his feet, walked out into the full light of day, looked into the face of the traveler, and said, "Yes, I am known for my wisdom. What is your question?"

"Wise old man, how can I become brilliant? Where can I find wisdom?"

The wise old guru stared for a moment into the weary traveler's anxious eyes and asked in reply, "Where can you find your horse?" And with that he turned and walked back into the cave.

The answer was obvious. The traveler's horse had been with him all the time; brilliance and the capacity for wisdom had been within him all the time.

Jesus said it: "The kingdom of God is within you" (Luke 17:21). God drops ideas into your mind every day like eggs in a nest. The first stage of faith is believing in yourself.

—◇—

Clean Out Your Closet

Unlock your private door. Here, in the sheltered safety of secure solitude, strip off the embarrassing, ill-fitting assortment of ideas you bought and closeted—ideas that now hang in your mind like old garments that no longer deserve the place you gave to them.

Some are ideas that were given to you and that you accepted unhesitatingly, too intimidated to reject or discard them. Others are ideas that you believed in passionately for a time but then lost interest in.

Now's the time to clear out all those mental hang-ups. Discard the outdated possibilities that you've allowed to oppressively over-crowd your imagination over the years. Strip away any extraneous ideas—even those that are good (and some of them are)—to make room for better and more beautiful dreams. Clear out the closet! You're free! Free to peruse and pursue fresh new dreams.

Today you're becoming a new you, and you've been given the best gift ever! You're invited to select a completely new wardrobe of dynamic ideas, positive possibilities. You can choose the style and size!

Yes, bravely do what you should have done long ago: reorganize your mental closet. But be careful! Wisely save the precious ideas that you should never discard. But clear out all the junk that still hangs in the crammed shadows of your soul—all those hang-ups, judgments, oppressive low-self-esteem complexes, and self-deprecating attitudes. Yes—out! Away! Gone!

A whole new mental wardrobe is needed.

◆

A New Energy Source

Careful. Don't waste creative energy through delays or careless distraction. Plan your time wisely. When you don't have a plan, the time can get away from you. Time gets lost without a schedule. That's why the old axiom still holds true, "If you want to get something done, give it to the busiest person you know."

A positive plan can unleash latent energy. When you have a plan, the excitement from working on the plan will create literally more energy than if you had no direction. Lethargy is a natural by-product of aimlessness. That's why people who get up one hour earlier to exercise report a greater amount of energy. They are able to do more and need to sleep less. They have taken good care of their bodies and have invested wisely in body energy.

A plan gives direction.

A dream gives energy.

—◇—

Plug In to God

Negative emotions such as doubt, fear, worry, anger, hostility, self-pity, and jealousy will drain you of your energy. Likewise, indecision saps energy. Commitment, on the other hand, taps into and releases incredible powers—physical, emotional, and spiritual. If you've got the faith, God's got the power. He wants to open floodgates of energy in the person who applies his faith and gets going. As you spend yourself building, constructing, helping, and pursuing great causes, you become tremendously enthusiastic. You don't consume energy; you recycle your energy supply!

—◆—

Enthusiasm Is Energy

Possibility Thinking is the great energy generator. For energy is generated by happy hopes and keen anticipations of interesting or exciting events. Remember when you were a child, the night before a picnic? How excited you were. How hard it was to get to sleep. How early you rose and bounded out of bed. Not long ago I was suffering from fatigue. I was in between projects. Then I began writing this book. I began to imagine the completed manuscript, the bound volume, and I have never had more energy than I have as I write this. No wonder that Possibility Thinkers always seem to have an abundance of energy. Hope-filled thinking produces great enthusiasm, and *enthusiasm is energy!*

Get the success cycle started now: (1) Get a possibility idea. (2) Imagine it. (3) Become enthusiastic. (4) Move ahead and you will experience great surges of energy.

Enthusiasm creates energy. Have you not seen it happen? I have, in many a committee meeting. The committee meets for the monthly meeting. They think they have nothing to talk about. But they begin to chat until out of the aimless conversation some creative idea is launched, picked up, elaborated, developed, analyzed, and the people who were lolling sleepily now sit upright. The hands that were lazily folded are now clasped excitedly, drowsy eyes are now alert, sparkling—wide awake!

—◆—

The Source of Youthful Energy

Possibility Thinking is the great source and secret of youthful energy. Why do we speak of youthful energy? Is it not because some young people, by virtue of their years, can see greater possibilities for achievement and service than a man who is calendar-old? This is the reason why young people without goals and dreams are really old and tired. They often are tempted to think immoral thoughts to create enough mental excitement and generate enough energy to really feel alive. This explains why some people in their eighties may demonstrate more energy than some twenty-year-olds. The eighty-year-old man with a constructive project has far more physical energy than the teenager who is aimless, causeless, project-less, and purposeless. Possibility Thinking generates energy. Impossibility Thinking generates fatigue. It is that simple.

So the Possibility Thinker, no matter how physically weary he feels at the moment, never responds to a positive idea with: "I'm too tired." Never! He responds with: "Is it a good idea?" And if he gets an affirmative answer to that question, he suddenly finds energy coming *mysteriously* from—he *doesn't know where!* It is the powerful presence of a spirit called "God" within him! The truth is, Possibility Thinkers are people who have discovered the secret and source of youthful energy.

Come Alive!

Possibility Thinkers are risk-running, chance-taking, high-adventure-seeking sanctified speculators. For they are more interested in service and success than they are in security. As a result they plunge when they see great potentials. Nerve and courage are the trademarks of their character. They have escaped the monotony that penalizes careful people with boredom, listlessness, and fatigue.

Some men die by shrapnel
And some go down in flames,
But most men perish inch by inch,
Playing at little games.

. . . One of the most energetic men who ever lived was Theodore Roosevelt. He was a daring Possibility Thinker who said, "Far better it is to dare mighty things, to win glorious triumphs, even though checkered by failure, than to take rank with those poor spirits who neither enjoy much nor suffer much, because they live in the gray twilight that knows not victory nor defeat."

Come alive! Find a dream. Pick a goal. Take on a project. You'll feel young again. Youthful energy will burst forth from the tomb of your half-dead body. You will be born again! This is God coming alive—really!—*in you!*

—◆—

Energize Your Dreams

What is enthusiasm? It is that mysterious something that turns an average person into an outstanding individual. It makes an old person young, and without it a young person becomes old. It is the hidden spring of endless energy. It is that beautiful force that carries us from mediocrity to excellence. It turns on a bright light in a dull face until the eyes sparkle and the personality brightens with joy. It is the spiritual magnet that attracts helpful and happy people to become our fruitful friends. It is the joyful emotional fountain that bubbles up, attracting persons to come to our side and drink from the joy that rises out of our heart. It is the happy song of a positive person who sings an inspiring message to the world: "I can! It's possible! We'll do it."

Enthusiasm is that long-sought-after fountain of eternal life. Old men stop to drink of its elixir and suddenly dream new dreams. Marvelous, miraculous, mysterious new strength surges through the old bones. Discouragement fades like the morning fog in the shining sun. Suddenly you catch yourself whistling, noticing birds flying, seeing the glorious shape of the white clouds against blue sky. From deep within yourself a new song breaks forth. You whistle. You sing. Now you are alive again!

———◇———

Enthusiasm Begets Energy

Whether climbing your mountain literally means climbing mountains like the Himalayas or climbing mountains of obstacles: Success depends on positive energy that enables you to stick with it.

Energy that is positive is energy fed by enthusiasm. Enthusiasm produces such positive energy that even when you're physically exhausted you can't wait to wake up the next morning to climb to a higher ledge. Positive energy moves you forward. Enthusiasm lifts you higher. Success becomes self-perpetuating.

Negative thinking fatigues you, but positive energy replenishes you. Positive energy becomes a self-propagating force that knows no end. You achieve a new peak experience and from the new peak experience you are so exhilarated that you become confident that you can do even more than you thought. You see a new peak, so you begin to reach for it. When you reach that peak you receive a larger vision. Call this peak-to-peak living. The larger vision releases more enthusiasm. The new enthusiasm releases more energy. And you have a success cycle going that nothing can stop.

Jesus Christ, come into my life. Flush all negative thinking out of my mind. Love people through me. I believe you are coming into me now in the form of God-filled ideas. I know I have enormous undiscovered, untapped energy within me. I feel young, I have energy, I am energetic. Thank you for this vitality and strength of mind and body. Live within me, O God, and do good works now through me. Thank you again. Amen.

No Enthusiasm Without Integrity

There can be no enthusiasm in anything that you are promoting, projecting, planning, or striving toward unless it has total integrity. How many people do you know who don't have enough enthusiasm! A major reason for this is that many people are not totally honest in their private lives. If you harbor dark, black secrets, or if you're not totally honest, you cannot be enthusiastic, for enthusiasm is the practice of emotional freedom. Guilty persons dare not be emotionally liberated. They must become emotionally restrained or they just might "let the cat out of the bag" and "expose their dishonesty."

So the person who isn't honest definitely develops a subconscious emotional shell around his deeper emotions. People who, at their core, are dishonest, phony, flaky, or synthetic develop an emotional personality that restrains them from being bubbly and open. They cultivate an icy, chilly shell around their emotional selves. This shelters them from becoming the totally open persons who could expose their phoniness. That's why the hypocrite can never be a joyous and happy success. He lacks emotional power and energy that comes from enthusiasm! So only honest persons develop naturally into sincerely enthusiastic people. Integrity therefore must be at the core of your life.

———◆———

Be Extraordinary

The word "enthusiasm" comes from the Greek words *en Theos*, which, freely translated, mean "in God." God flows into human lives through constructive, creative ideas. God's ideas flowing through human minds are always aimed at revealing and realizing our undetected or underdeveloped potential. And enthusiasm is stimulated when the human mind is invaded by an idea that challenges it to grow. I believe that God structured the enthusiasm-generating system this way because God knows every living human being should be doing more than he's doing, thinking bigger than he's thinking, and planning more than he's planning. God knows that every living human being, whether he's four years old or ninety years old, still has to battle against the temptation to be lazy, to play it safe and avoid risks.

Growing is a part of life. There can be no stimulation unless there is the capacity for growth. This growth may be in quality, but growth potential must exist. Growth is essential, and that means the idea must be extraordinary. I'm sure that a mountain climber who has scaled a twenty-four-thousand-foot peak would no longer be excited by a foothill in California.

The capacity to be extraordinary—a little more or a little better than last time—is a quality that fosters and causes the flow of divine enthusiasm.

Choose the best; shun mediocrity. Mediocrity has a way of shriveling up enthusiasm. But commitment to excellence taps an incredible source of energy. Elect the best, no matter what the price tag.

—◇—

God's Ideas

Show me a person who's really dynamic and alive with exciting energy and I'll show you a person who's turned on by God's ideas. God's ideas are loaded with far more possibilities than we ever suspected. When we are in God and God is within us, then fantastic ideas come to us. His ideas are loaded with possibilities. These possibilities stimulate us with great positive expectations. No wonder our enthusiasm never dries up. And we have, in fact, tapped into an energy power that can and will see us all the way to the top of the mountain.

What's really surprising is how God used even the minds of persons who may call themselves atheists. "I've never experienced God," Gorbachev once said to me. "You are wrong!" I answered, "God was in your heart, mind, and spirit when He chose to give you the concept and the courage to bring peace and freedom to your nation."

—◆—

Feed Your Enthusiasm

Enthusiasm—what is it? How do you explain this mountain-melting power? How can you get it? I'll say it *again:* The word comes from two Greek words *"en"* and *"Theos."* Literally translated they mean "in God." We speak of such persons as inspired. *In-Spirited* people! Fill your life with the God Spirit and all kinds of power break forth. In the words of an ancient Hebrew prophet, "The zeal of the Lord will perform it."

Feed your life with a happy positive faith and you'll find yourself:

- uncovering great opportunities;

- discovering beautiful solutions;

- overcoming impossible obstacles;

- unwrapping surprises God has in store for you;

- rolling back the dark clouds, until sunlight breaks through.

That's enthusiasm. How can you get it? How do you feed it? By filling your mind with a positive mental attitude—that's how! Positive thinking is the very life of God working itself in our brains.

◇

Check Your Sails

You're at a real testing time. Here you confront a loss of enthusiasm. Your energy level is at a dangerous low. The strong winds of passion that have been driving you are no longer filling your sails. You aren't moving ahead anymore. "What should I do?" you ask. Look up and check the sky sails.

"All sails are set, sir." Many a captain heard that glad sound in the glorious heyday of ocean-going clippers.... During the storms—the trying times we all face—a wise old captain would know that it's not how hard the wind blows that matters, but how strong the mast is and how firmly the sails are tied down.

Then there are the dead seas, with nary a breath of wind. The sails hang limp. The vigorous surge of a fully wind-blown ship is dead. The calm is deadening. Progress is delayed.

Wise captains plan for delays that are out of their control. Look how the old China clippers were designed. First there were the *gallant sails,* large and strong, to catch the full power of a strong wind. Above them were set smaller sails to catch higher breezes; these were called the *royal sails.* But above the gallant sails and the royal sails were the *sky sails*—small and light. Tied to the very top of the tall masts, they were designed to catch the smallest wisp of wind, the slightest, lightest, highest breeze. Although they'd never deliver enough thrust to take the great China clipper across the ocean, they too served a lifesaving purpose: they were enough to keep a calmed vessel from drifting off course.

Again and again it was the sky sails that saved the ship in deadening delays. They didn't move the ship to its port, but they kept the vessel on its course.

—◆—

Possibilities Unlimited

I can count
the seeds in an apple.
But, Lord—you alone
can count the apples
in one seed!
Some things are
impossible, Lord!
It's impossible for me
to see the immeasurable, unlimited
possibilities in one
fertile idea.
Praise the Lord.
Amen.

———◇———

Untapped Possibilities

On one occasion, while traveling from Iowa to California, we watched the endless acres of fertile Iowa farmland move past our car window. It is a majestic sight to see rising from the good earth a healthy and heavy harvest of grain and corn. Not an acre is wasted. Every piece of land is put to good use. After the fruitful plains we reached the bleak and barren foothills of the great Rocky Mountains. These rugged peaks greet the traveler like granite sentinels standing guard at the gateway to the Pacific. We began to climb the twisting road that winds like a snake up the hillside. Finally we reached a point where we could look to the west and see the beautiful but unproductive mountains and to the east where unfolding below on the endless plains was the rich farmland with little lakes and rivers shimmering in the scene. What a contrast! I stopped for gas and, pointing to the mountains, made the mistake of saying to the station attendant, "What a lot of worthless land!" That fine young man whirled around, looked at me with fire in his eyes, and firmly corrected me with these words, "That is *not* wasteland. There are minerals in those rocks, and there may be oil. We believe there is uranium too. We just haven't found it yet."

Men and women also have untapped possibilities to achieve success in life where often, at first glance, it appears there are none. "You are the salt of the earth. . . . You are the light of the world," Jesus Christ said to the motley crowd gathered on the mountain to hear Him preach. "You are somebody!"

Undetected Possibilities

To Jesus every problem was a possibility in disguise.

Sickness was an opportunity for healing. Sin was an opportunity for forgiveness. Sorrow was an opportunity for compassion. Personal abuse was an opportunity to leave a good impression and show the world how Possibility Thinkers react!

To Jesus every person was a gold mine of undiscovered, hidden possibilities! . . .

To Jesus the important fact about you and me is not that we are sinners, but that we can be saints. So Jesus proclaimed the greatest possibility: the immeasurable mercy of God.

To Jesus the whole world was jammed, pregnant, loaded, bulging with untapped, undiscovered, undetected possibilities! Jesus really believed in the supreme spiritual *possibilities!*

Man *can* be born again! Character *can* be changed! You *can* become a new person! Life *can* be beautiful! There *is* a solution to every problem! There *is* a light behind every shadow!

Yes! Jesus had an unshakable faith in these ultimate spiritual possibilities:

God exists!

Life goes on beyond death!

Heaven is for real!

Jesus was prepared to prove it. By dying—and rising again!

Jesus was impressed by what the world could become—never depressed by what the world was.

He truly believed that common people can become uncommonly powerful. He knew without a shadow of a doubt that ordinary persons could become Possibility Thinkers.

———◇———

A Possibility in Disguise

An interesting thing happened to me one morning on the way to my office. I was driving an old car that I had bought seven years earlier. It's been such a faithful old car. A few miles from our church I looked at the speedometer and watched the little odometer blocks change: 99,999.5 . . . 99,999.6 . . . 99,999.7 . . . 99,999.8 . . . 99,999.9. Then it read 00,000.0. I had a brand-new car! It sat in the parking lot all day with only three miles on it.

Now we all know that you cannot tell the newness of a car by the mileage gauge, just as you can't tell a book by its cover. It's not a new car just because the gauge reads 00,000.0. It can't be re-created into a brand-new car. But we—as humans—can become new persons. We can be "born again."

You become a new person when you learn one of life's most important lessons: every problem is a possibility in disguise. Every impossibility is a fantastic opportunity, an opportunity to start a business; improve your business; start a new career; start a new relationship; repair a neglected relationship; invent a new product; grow spiritually (It's a decision! Just do it.); learn your faults, things that your ego has long blinded you from seeing; or, be alone to reflect, meditate, and think things through, or? . . . or? . . . or?

Whatever you do, remember: nothing new happens until some creative person tackles an impossible situation! Today's impossibilities are tomorrow's breakthroughs. Progress never starts until someone challenges a long-standing impossibility. Climbing a mountain? Trying to reach your peak? Facing an impossibility? Good! God is just trying to motivate you. You haven't begun to discover your real potential.

Intimidated by the Mountain

How do you handle an impossibility? You are *intimidated* by an impossibility when (1) you do nothing because you fear failure; (2) you do nothing because you are afraid of criticism; (3) you do nothing because you are uncertain of success; (4) you do nothing because you're afraid of the cost; (5) you do nothing because you can't be sure of perfection; (6) you do nothing about this beautiful, impossible idea because you see something about it that's not right (there's something wrong with the best idea); (7) you do nothing because you're not sure you'd get credit for success if you managed to make it.

To be intimidated means that you come up against a mountain and say "it's impossible to climb." The massive peak overpowers and silences you. So you withdraw, you give up, you're intimidated by the mountain. . . .

Impossibilities intimidate and stop some people yet illuminate and motivate others. Get turned on by an impossibility! Don't be intimidated by it!

Albert Einstein was once asked, "How did you discover relativity?" His answer was, "I questioned and challenged an axiom."

Do you want to know the secret of success? Ask any successful person and he will say, "I refused to be intimidated by an impossibility. I was motivated to challenge the impossibility!" If impossibilities intimidate you, then you are a loser. If impossibilities motivate you, you are a winner already!

AUGUST 8

———◇———

Foolish Limitations

A tourist walked down a pier and watched a fisherman pull in a large fish, measure it, and throw it back. He caught a second fish, smaller this time, measured it, and put it in his bucket. Oddly, all the large fish that he caught that measured ten inches or more he discarded. All fish smaller than ten inches he kept. Puzzled, the curious onlooker questioned, "Pardon me, but why do you keep the little ones and throw the big ones away?" The old fellow looked up and without blinking an eye said, "Why, because my frying pan measures only ten inches across!"

Foolish? Of course. But no more so than when you throw away the biggest ideas and the most beautiful dreams that come into your mind simply because your experience is too limited, your self-confidence too undeveloped to enable you to grab hold of the big opportunities God sends your way!

Start growing now. Think big. Big things happen to big-thinking people. Nothing big happens to little-thinking people.

---◇---

Ask Smart Questions

Life's not fair—why is it that way? "Why do bad things happen to good people?" is a question often raised. My answer? That's the wrong question. It's wrong because no one knows the answer. "Why" is the question God never will answer. When we ask "Why" we don't want an explanation—we want an argument. We want to argue when we don't want to accept. Life's unfair—that's a given—not a debate.

Likewise, God never answers the questions that begin with "When?" Such as, "When will this injustice cease? When will I be treated fairly?" Again and again in the Old Testament the people of God, in their suffering, cried out, "How long, O Lord? Before You deliver us?" And never—never did God answer.

Ask smart questions, like: "What" will I do about this? Like: "What" are my options? Like: "What" do I have left? Like: "How" shall I respond? Will my reaction to what's happened make matters better or worse? Will it attract strong and good support? Can I turn this obstacle into an opportunity? Is there some good that could possibly come out of this bad scene? Is this a final defeat—or a temporary setback? Am I "finished"? If so, I'll choose the final finish—with a glow!

Don't Surrender to the Negative

One morning a distraught parishioner telephoned [Bishop] Phillips Brooks. This emotionally devastated man was one of Boston's most prestigious professionals. "Pastor, have you seen the morning paper? I'm ruined!" Then he told the story to Bishop Brooks.

When he finished, the pastor said, "Well, first, I didn't read the morning paper. I never do. More than half the people in the town never do. They only read the late afternoon paper.

"Second, of the people who get the paper, only a fraction will read this section.

"Third, the people who read it will be your friends or your enemies. Don't worry about your enemies; they're not on your side anyway. And the friends who read it? The wise and thoughtful people in this group won't believe it. They'll be on the line to defend you before you know it! Yes, in your heart you have been hurt by this. But ruined?! No way!"

Don't surrender leadership of your life to negative facts, negative faces, negative fears—or a negative faith. Negative faith?! Yes, faith can be positive or negative. Negative faith is believing that God is angry with you. Negative faith is assuming you are being punished for your sins. Reject this destructive notion. God takes no pleasure in seeing you suffer.

God loves you and is way ahead of you in planning and preparing to save and strengthen you!

When Life Hands You Hurts . . .

Listen to the caring voices you have never heard before. Be open to the possibility that there is a living, loving God. God may be trying to connect with you to help you with a burst of faith that you have never before been willing to consider as a reality. There are so many worlds within worlds, and the best and brightest of us have never been exposed to many of the realities of this spiritual universe. . . . Since your birth this Eternal Super Spirit called God has made and is making millions of moves to connect with your spirit.

Look and listen to the positive ideas, moods, emotions, impulses, memories, and mental assumptions that are constantly entering your consciousness. Whatever stimulates your sense of aliveness could well be a message from God. Or the aliveness could be the very presence of God within you!

The Bible claims to present the voice and word of God to humans on planet earth. Here we read: "Lo, I am with you always" (Matt. 28:20). God can inspire and inject ideas into your mind or feelings into your heart.

With six billion humans on earth, God has six billion possible humans to use in his network of communicating to other persons. So long as we can see, hear, notice, and be influenced (however slightly) by another human, we may be getting a message from the God who knows all, cares compassionately, and is making connections to our hearts, minds, and spirits, even if we don't attribute any life or credit to Him. Be open to see and hear God in anything or anyone.

—◇—

When Life Hands You Hurts . . .

See your hurt as a process, not as an event. The hurt has not happened; it is *happening.* The outline of this painful scene will change shape as the hours, days, weeks, months, and years unfold. Therefore, it is all-important for you to understand that your reaction, more than anything else, will shape the force and the face of this initial pain that hits you.

That's why positive affirmations are all-important. Try thinking, *I can diminish the negative impact of this hurt on my life.* Or, *I can change my hurt until it changes from an enemy into a helpful friend.*

I can turn my hurt into my halo! People will see God in me as I go through my poem!

Change is inevitable. You change. The world around you changes. Your circle of acquaintances and friends changes.

Your perspective of the whole painful experience will also change! Your needs will change. Your desires will change. It is absolutely certain that your perception of the hurt is in a process that is on the move! Believe that!

Remember Jesus' promise: "If you have faith as a mustard seed, your mountain will *move,* and nothing will be impossible for you" (Matt. 17:20, author's paraphrase).

---◇---

When Life Hands You Hurts . . .

Ask the question, What's the worst that can happen? Believe that, with all your positive-thinking faith, you'll be able to handle the worst! For the worst has been faced by thousands, perhaps millions, of other positive-thinking human beings before you. They were not overwhelmed by this "worst," and often they overwhelmed the worst when it hit. So will you if the worst really happens, only to collide with a positive Spiritual Power inside you!

"God sends no more hurt than we can bear" is the testimony of millions of persons who have experienced horrific hurts.

But what humans cannot handle is a mystery. So take your pain and fear out of the unreliable realm of negative fantasy and exaggerated imagination by asking the question, What's the worst that can happen? Face this prospect, for you as a God-inspired human are more than a match for the worst! You can, after all, face death, as we all surely will one day, and we're ready for that because our Leader and Lord, Jesus Christ, showed us how to get through that valley!

—◇—

Think First!

In our busy world we don't take time enough to "think." An experienced commercial pilot sat with me one day on a transcontinental flight. "Did you ever have any problems or crises? And how did you handle them?" I asked.

"Oh, yes," he said, "I've had a few. But when I was a pilot in the military, I learned 'In a potentially catastrophic emergency, don't do anything! Just think! Don't touch a single control! *Just think!*'"

He continued, "I was in the group that had the task of bombing Tokyo Bay during World War II. In a dive preparing to drop my bomb load, I was hit by incoming fire. I thought for a moment that I was finished. But I did nothing! I can't tell you how difficult it was to resist grabbing the controls. All I did was *think,* and my thought was, *I believe I'm on a correct pattern. I'll come out of this.* And in fact the controls were set for me to come out of the dive, and I did. Had I done anything at all to throw the control pattern off, I would have been finished!"

So when your moods take a nosedive, don't do anything—just think! And wait! And of course fill your mind with prayer and positive thoughts. You will master your moods. And it will make the difference between success and failure—believe me!

Oh, how hard it is to resist the temptation to lunge into action when you have run into disaster. Yet the first step to survival is this: *do nothing!*

◆

To Face Difficulties

Truly, Father, all things work together for good to those who love you.

Thank you for the difficulties that produce divine dividends.

I know that pain is only a phase of the growing process: that seed buried alive under suffocating ground in a windowless grave agonizes before it ruptures into new life.

I know that I build hard muscles in heart, mind, and body only when I lift heavy loads. I thank you for tough times that produce calluses that could save my spirit from softness that would be weakness.

There have been times, O Lord, when only through great difficulty have I learned the valuable lessons. I was too blind to see, too arrogant to believe, or too stubborn to accept any other way than by a bed of pain.

I praise you for the times an open door slammed in my face and forced me out of an old rut that I never would have had the courage to leave, and led me down the road to a beautiful new life.

I thank you for heartbreak which caused me to bury the hatchet and speak again to someone with whom I had for far too long been out of touch.

Thank you, Father, for life's priceless times of fruitful difficulty. Amen.

—◇—

There's Always a Way
When You Really Try

We have several walnut trees on our church grounds. California crows love the meat of the walnut. How can a crow crack a walnut to get at the meat? Imagine if you were a crow—how would you do it? The crows have figured out a way. They pick the walnut up in their bills, fly high over our church parking lot, and let the nuts fall on the hard surface! The walnuts crack—and the clever birds swoop down and eat the meat! If a crow's brain can find a solution to its problem, surely you'll be able to solve yours.

—◇—

Success in Two Easy Steps

To really succeed in life, all you have to do is (1) get started and (2) never quit. Those are the only two hurdles you need to clear to become the person God wants you to be!

Let me call your attention to a powerful Bible verse: "For [God] says: 'In an acceptable time I have heard you, / And in the day of salvation I have helped you.' / Behold, now is the accepted time; behold, now is the day of salvation" (2 Cor. 6:2).

You didn't think when you got up this morning that this would be the day your life would change, did you? But it's going to happen because the only things that stand between you and grand success in living are . . . *getting started* and *never quitting!* You can solve your biggest problem by getting started, right here and now.

———◇———

Cast All Your Anxieties on Him

What sufferings, setbacks, slaps, insults, or injustices are you holding on to? What negative comment did a high school or elementary teacher make about you that has held you back? What label did you accept that now keeps you from even trying to break out of the mold that someone who really didn't know you put you in? . . .

What unhealthy comments are you holding on to? Was it something your spouse said? Or was it your overly critical mother or demanding father? Perhaps someone told you, "You are *never* good enough" or "You *always* overreact."

Get rid of it! Get over it! Give it up—to God!

"Cast all your anxieties on Him!"

What secret are you holding on to that you are so afraid someone will discover? Who will discover it—your spouse? your parents? your children? your boss? What sins have you committed that have yet to be exposed and forgiven, or for which you have yet to forgive yourself?

Give it up—to Jesus Christ!

"Cast all your anxieties on Him."

Only one leader of any religious movement had scars in the palms of both hands. He is the only person who claimed to be sent by God with the authority to forgive people for their sins. Give your baggage to Him.

◆

A Prayer for Solutions

Lord, thanks for assuring me that you'll solve the problems
if I'll exercise the faith and make the right decision!
Forgive me for waiting for all difficulties, real or fanciful,
to be resolved before deciding to make my commitment.
I confess I have too often allowed problems
instead of possibilities to take over the leadership of my life—to
make my decisions—and take command over my destiny.
I know, now, what faith is, Lord!
It's making the right decisions before I see solutions
to all the problems!
Increase my faith!
Amen.

—◇—

Give It All Away

There is a legend of a man who was lost in the desert, dying of thirst. He stumbled on until he came to an abandoned house. Outside the dilapidated, windowless, weather-beaten, deserted shack was a pump. He stumbled forward and began pumping furiously, but no water came from the well. Then he noticed a small jug with a cork at the top and a note written on the side: "You have to prime the pump with water, my friend. P.S. And fill the jug again before you leave." He pulled out the cork and saw that the jug was full of water.

Should he pour it down the pump? What if it didn't work? All of the water would be gone. If he drank the water from the jug, he could be sure he would not die of thirst. But to pour it down the rusty pump on the flimsy instruction written on the outside of the jug?

Something told him to follow the advice and choose the risky decision. He proceeded to pour the whole jug of water down the rusty old pump and furiously pumped up and down. Sure enough, the water gushed out! He had all he needed to drink. He filled the jug again, corked it, and added his own words beneath the instructions on the jug: "Believe me, it really works. You have to give it all away before you can get anything back."

The principle was well stated by the apostle Paul: "He who sows sparingly will also reap sparingly, and he who sows bountifully will also reap bountifully" (2 Cor. 9:6).

If you want to succeed, you have to "go for it" and give it all you've got.

—◇—

The Secret of Success

Success is an unselfish goal, while failure is a selfish goal. It is impossible to succeed without helping a lot of people along the way. The secret of success is simple: find a hurt and heal it; find a problem and solve it; find an obstacle and remove it, bridge it, or turn it into an opportunity.

———◇———

Unlimited Dreams

What goals would you be setting for yourself if you knew you could not fail?

What dreams would you have on the drawing board if you knew you would ultimately succeed—in the long run?

What plans would you be making if you had thirty years to carry them out?

What projects would you be launching if you had the wisdom to solve any problem and the power to sweep all obstacles out of your way?

What exciting work would you be engaged in today if you could acquire the skill to sell your ideas to powerful people?

What role should you play in the drama of human life? Clarify your role before you set your goal or you'll encounter confusion and frustration. Conflict in interpersonal relations is too often the result of a misinterpretation by the involved persons of the roles each should be playing.

Here's a simple formula for success: Role → Goal + Toll = SUCCESS. Define your role; then, and then only, get set to establish your goal. Be prepared to pay the price in terms of time, money, energy, and credit-sharing, and you'll succeed.

—◆—

Believe in Success

I can tell you what God's plan for your life is in general terms. This is a universal principle. God wants to use you to do something beautiful in the world around you. That's it in one sincere sentence. God created you and allowed you to be born because He wanted to use you where you are . . .

To find a hurt and heal it

To find somebody with a problem and help him solve it

To find someone who's trapped and help him discover liberty and freedom

To find someone who is defeated and lift him up again and give him new hope and a new dream

So believe in success and choose to succeed. For you're bound to help someone along the way. It's impossible to succeed without being a servant to someone. So believe that you can succeed if you really want to!

God can do great things through the person who doesn't care who gets the credit.

—◇—

S-U-C-C-E-S-S

Anyone who wants to succeed can do so. Success can take many forms. It may be recovering from surgery or rebuilding your body after an accident. It may be starting a new life after a torturous experience of rejection and divorce. It may be pursuing a new career at the age of sixty-five. Whatever it is, you can succeed.

Believe in success. What do we mean by success? *Success is building self-esteem in yourself and others through sacrificial service to God and to your fellow human beings.* You may accumulate riches, fame, and honors, but unless you achieve tremendous self-esteem in the process, all that the world calls success becomes ashes in your hands.

The secret of success is to find a need and fill it.

S-U-C-C-E-S-S

S—Select your goal.

U—Unlock your positive thinking.

C—Chart your course.

C—Commit yourself.

E—Expect problems and difficulties.

S—Sacrifice yourself.
(Yes, success always involves a cross!)

S—Stick with it.
(You never fail until you say, "I quit.")

It all spells *success!*
Believe that you can and will succeed!

A Prayer for Success

As I become a success with your help, Lord,
let me never forget that what I am
is more important than what I do.
Faith stimulates success.
Hope sustains success.
Love sanctifies success.
So I cannot and I dare not succeed
without your power, peace,
and pressure in my life, Jesus Christ.
Amen.

Be open. Be humble. Correctable. Educable. Then you will hear God's voice. You will see God's plan. Grab onto it, give it all you've got, and you will inherit the earth!

—◇—

Imagine Success

Success? It does not happen without total aliveness generated only by a revitalized imagination. The developer imagines the structures rising—with fountains, steel, glass, escalators, and elevators! . . .

The father and mother imagine a home of their own. They clip pictures out of magazines. They pore over illustrations of furniture. They look at baby furniture and children's clothes and imagine a family!

The salesman imagines the faces of his customers lighting up with excitement to buy his product and service because it's just what they need. . . .

The manager imagines defensive faces of workers changing shape to become receptive, welcoming and appreciating and accepting his supervision.

The financier imagines a small dollar base growing larger, slowly, then a bit faster, then pyramiding, until, with incredible speed, his resources multiply and his fortunes inflate! He is now positioned for joyous philanthropy!

The athlete imagines her body responding to exercise and fitness routines until the mirror reflects an amazing profile! Now she imagines running swiftly, like an elk, like a greyhound, like a fox. She imagines jumping over the wall—high, higher—clearing the bar, breaking the limit! Bells ring. The applause is deafening. She did it! She really did it!

Success is never-ending and failure is never final to that person who knows how to revitalize and renew the God-given powers of creative imagination.

—◆—

Budget Your Time

Start a time budget. This begins with a plan. Plan your day and work your plan. We have all had frustrating times when we planned our day and we tried to work our plan—only to have unforeseeable interruptions. As a result, we may be tempted to give up and simply head into every day without a plan. Nothing could be more disastrous as far as your time budget is concerned. Unaccountable loss is inevitable. You will end up talking too long on the telephone, and compulsively spending your time in nonconstructive ways.

Make a written list of what you would *like* to do today, what you *can* do today, what you *must* do today. Now make a priority list. List first things first. Allocate your first minutes to those opportunities that may never come again. This will often take priority over what you think you "must" do. You will be surprised to find that many things you think you must do can actually wait.

Be prepared to defend your plan for the day. Discipline yourself against the temptation to top your priority list with what you would like to do. Strong self-discipline is required as you plot your day. Be prepared to say "No" to yourself and to others who might want to spend your time unwisely. You may have to take the telephone off the hook, or ignore the doorbell. Learn to say "No" in a fair, friendly, frank, and firm manner.

—◇—

Balance Your Time Budget

Balance your time budget by your value judgments. More than one man has made a million dollars by working sixteen hours a day seven days a week for many years only to lose his wife and watch his children grow up and leave before he realized what was happening. Don't make the mistake of spending so much time pursuing your ambition that you join the ranks of those who are rich, but lonely; wealthy, but dead. The health of the body, mind, soul, and family requires that time be balanced wisely.

Remember that God created the human being with specific instructions to spend one day in seven for the rest and re-creation of the soul and the body. Re-creation of the body comes through re-creation of the spirit. It is no coincidence that a vast number of the truly successful people in our world are also leaders in their churches or synagogues.

An anonymous Irishman wrote:

Take time for work, it is the price of success.
Take time to think, it is the source of power.
Take time to play, it is the secret of youth.
Take time to read, it is the foundation of wisdom.
Take time to be friendly, it is the road to happiness.
Take time to dream, it's hitching your wagon to a star.
Take time to love, it is the highest joy of life.
Take time to laugh, it is the music of the soul.

AUGUST 29

◆

Be Prepared for Interruptions

By all means, budget some time for delays and interruptions. The man who has an income of five hundred dollars a month is headed for financial trouble if he has nothing budgeted for unforeseen expenses. Likewise, many people fail in time management because they fail to budget time for unavoidable emergencies. "Always allow time for a flat tire whenever you are going somewhere," my dad wisely told me. I still do.

No two words will do more to solve time problems than: *start early*. Repairmen, deliverymen, and servicemen will promise you that you may expect something at a certain time. Unless they have a long-standing reputation for punctuality, you will be wise in allowing, in your time budget, time for delays. If you do not, delays can prove costly indeed in missed appointments and even more expensive in the toll of destructive emotions inflicted on your mind and body.

Allow for delays and it may save your life on the highway—or your grade at the end of the semester—or your reputation with an important businessman with whom you have an appointment. Allow for no delays and you may become irritated, aggravated, and angry, all of which are destructive emotions.

◈

Delays Are Opportunities
in Disguise

Time spent allowing for delays and actual delays themselves can be used creatively. A friend of mine named Harry Johnson drives the freeway. He always carries a book with him, and when there is an accident and he is hopelessly tied up in traffic, he reads his book. Last year, using his waiting freeway moments wisely, he read three books. I suppose this is also a comment on our California freeways.

My friend Maurice Te Paske was the mayor of Sioux Center, Iowa. He sent every citizen of that town a birthday card. How did he find time? Well, he took these cards along to meetings where his presence was required. When time was being eaten up by trivia which did not deserve or expect his attention, you could see the mayor signing his birthday cards.

Many Possibility Thinkers accomplish the seemingly impossible—thanks to delays that they know will come. They plan for them. They use the time profitably. A delay is often a rare opportunity to impress people. It's a chance to build a great reputation as a patient and understanding person.

◆

Weigh Your Time Carefully

Not all hours are of equal "weight." An hour early in the day is more valuable than an hour late in the afternoon. An hour in the spring is more powerful than an hour in the humid summer. An hour on Monday may invariably find you at less than your best, while an hour on Wednesday may be an hour that normally finds you in your highest, most alive, and most dynamic spirit. Discover which hours of what days are the highest and best for you. This will vary from person to person depending on a variety of factors including geography, climate, profession, and season. In Alaska, where the days are short in winter, and the darkness long, a person's emotional life will differ from the emotional life of a person who is living in Acapulco, Mexico. Find the hours of the day, the days of the week, the months of the year when you are at your highest efficiency. Plan, as much as possible, your most important work to fall in your best hours and your best months. . . .

Many creative people have discovered that the early morning and the very late hours are their best hours. This may be due to the fact that their subconscious mind is relaxed since it anticipates no interruptions at these unearthly hours. A creative mind produces its most fertile thoughts in periods of deep relaxation.

Weigh your hours. And you will discover that by reorganizing you can put the biggest jobs in the best time spots and can accomplish far more than you are accomplishing today.

SEPTEMBER 1

—◆—

Create Your Own Time Pressures

To protect yourself against the temptation to postpone and delay your projects, create your own pressure system. . . .

Low achievers have a habit of safely protecting themselves from the pressures of schedules by not making them. The truth is that you may have to follow concrete steps to force yourself to action.

1. Pick a concrete goal you hope to reach. If you don't, you will spend all of your life filing, looking through the file for what you filed, reading and filing some more, studying and researching and filing your observations, preparing reports on what you have filed and what you have researched, making indexes to your files and carbon copies for all members of the office, etc., etc., etc. . . . The only way to escape the trap of trivial time-consuming activity is to have in front of you a very specific, precise objective.

2. Set a deadline for reaching your goal.

3. Publicize your intentions and time-schedule to family, friends, and associates. This takes nerve. You run the risk of embarrassment if you do not make your goal or keep your schedule.

4. Once you have picked the goal, set a timetable for its achievement, and publicized it, you have created pressure on yourself. Result? You will get the job done! If not exactly in the announced time—shortly thereafter.

Make Time

Never reject and abandon your God-inspired dream by declaring, "I don't have the time." You don't, perhaps—but God does. *So let go and let God!* Your schedule will need to be reorganized to make the time to turn new mountains into marvelous miracles. . . .

Learn how to retire selectively from those duties you've always done. *Focus on the role where you're irreplaceable.* You'll be surprised at how well, wisely, and fruitfully your time will then be managed.

Yes, you can find time if you learn *how*, and *when*, and *from what* you must retire. It's easy to say goodbye if you have a higher, holier invitation to a new hello!

Lord, help me to know when to say good-bye and when to say hello. And give me the wisdom to make the transition with grace, courage, and kindness. Amen.

Make the time to allow bigger, better, and more beautiful things to happen.

How Do You Know
If You Don't Try?

One mile from my office in the Crystal Cathedral in California is Disneyland—a fabulous success story. Few people ever demonstrated more self-reliance than its founder, Walt Disney. How did he get it?

"When I was nearly twenty-one years old I went broke for the first time," Disney recalled before his death. "I slept on cushions from an old sofa and ate cold beans out of a can. Then I set out for Hollywood." Reflecting on his subsequent success, the Grand Man of Movieland uttered this priceless statement, "I didn't know what I couldn't do so I was willing to take a chance and try anything."

Walt Disney liked to tell the story of the boy who wanted so much to march in the circus parade. When the show came to town the bandmaster needed a trombonist, so the boy signed up. He hadn't marched a block when his horrible sounds created pandemonium. "Why didn't you tell me you couldn't play a trombone?" the bandmaster demanded. The boy answered simply, "How did I know? I never tried before!"

Get to Work

Possibility Thinking isn't just dreaming. *It's faith in action.* That translates into W-O-R-K with a patient commitment to excellence.

Check out the achievers: students, athletes, salespersons, educators, bankers, entrepreneurs, scientists, businesspersons, professional career persons (in medicine, law, the ministry). All achievers are achievers because they love to work!

Work. W-O-R-K. Connect this concept to the knowledge that timing is everything, and you realize that at every level, and at every stage in the process of pressing to achieve your goals, you must *work—harder, longer, and smarter.*

Facing problems? *Get back to work!*

—◇—

Buy a Red Shirt

A young boy approached a wealthy contractor standing on the sidewalk surveying the tall office structure he was building. "Tell me, sir," the boy asked, "how can I be successful like you when I grow up?" The gray-haired builder smiled kindly then spoke in the tough language of his trade, "Easy son. Buy a red shirt and work like crazy." Knowing that the youngster didn't understand, the wealthy builder of skyscrapers explained, pointing to the skeleton of his rising new structure, "See all those men up there? See that man in the red shirt? I don't even know his name. But I've been noticing how hard he works. One of these days I'm going to need a new superintendent. I'll go to that fellow and say—'Hey you in the red shirt—come here!' He'll get the big opportunity!"

Remember: Most people fail, not because they lack talent, money, or opportunity; they fail because they never really planned to succeed. Plan your future because you have to live there!

A Simple Formula

The mathematics of high achievement can be stated by a simple formula. Begin with a dream. *Divide* the problems and conquer them one by one. *Multiply* the exciting possibilities in your mind. *Subtract* all negative thoughts to get started. *Add* enthusiasm. Your answer will be the attainment of your goal.

Select a Goal

If you aim at nothing, you'll hit nothing. If your goals are vague, your achievements will be vague. But if your decisions are specific, you will harvest specific results. . . .

Then select the right goal. Have you heard of the company that developed a new dog food? All the necessary nutrients—protein, minerals, fats, and carbohydrates—were included in the product. The company came out with a brand-new package and a national advertising program which included full-page ads and ingenious commercials. Everything was planned and designed to be a success.

After six months' sales, which had started slowly, dwindled to nothing. The chairman of the board called all the district sales managers together in a major meeting in Chicago.

"What's wrong?" he asked. "Look at the beautiful full-page ads we have in national magazines. Look at the expensive commercials on television."

He held up a box of the dog food and pointed to the back of the box. He read the contents and admired the beautiful packaging. "The cost is even lower than our competitors," he added. "Now tell me why you people aren't selling this dog food?"

You could hear a pin drop. Then someone at the back of the room slowly came to his feet and said, "Sir, the dogs don't like it."

The secret of success cannot be found by sitting in an expensive leather chair in a plush office and dreaming your dreams. The secret of success is to select a goal by finding a need and filling it. Find a hurt and heal it. Find a problem and help solve it.

251

---◆---

Stay Focused

What is your goal? Is it God's goal for you? Does it draw you like a magnet? Does it have meaning? Will it help others who are hurting?

If the answer to all of the above questions is *yes*, then be prepared to say *no* to propositions that will distract you from your goal. Saying *yes* always involves saying *no*. If you want to get in better physical shape, you may have to say *no* to overeating. If you want to save your marriage, you may have to say *no* to many distractions. Remember your goal and focus on it at all times.

Keeping your *focus* on your goal is easier when you have someone to help you. You may get tired. You will want to quit. Set aside quiet time, reflective time, refreshment time—not just for your body but for your soul. Get linked up with a positive church. That's the best place to find supportive people as well as a time and place to get in touch with your biggest support system—the God who made you and loves you. God must be a part of your goal, the bedrock on which to build your dream and to follow your goal to fruition.

—◇—

The Challenges That Confront You

Remember this: in setting your goals, bloom where you are planted.

Your mental attitude toward the spot you're in at any moment is all-important. If you think it's impossible, then your biggest problem is *you!* If you "think possibilities," you'll realize that every difficulty is a call to some personal triumph.

When you have invented a solution to a difficult problem or adjusted to a trying situation, you will know the high and happy feeling that comes when you experience personal triumph.

Once, while I was driving through the desert, the tire on my car went flat. I jacked up the rear end of the car and just managed to get the tire off when the jack broke and the car fell on its axle. I was stranded. No way now to raise the car.

"Wait a minute! Let's dig a hole," my wife suggested. So we did. Fortunately, I was off the pavement and on the shoulder. Indeed it was about as hard as cement. But with the tire wrench I chipped away! Stone by stone, pebble by pebble, I labored on until I had dug a hole deep enough to take the flat tire off and drop the spare tire into—and onto the waiting bolts! Did I ever feel the exhilaration of a personal triumph! Every problem can become a personal triumph, making life a real adventure from beginning to end!

If you never challenge personal problems, you'll never be able to taste the exhilaration of a personal triumph! Remember: *triumph* is made up of two words: *try* and *umph*.

———◇———

Consider the Values You Live By

I was shocked to learn that an ex-convict read my book on Possibility Thinking and was inspired to plot an unbelievable holdup! He was thinking possibilities, but the wrong kind.

What is all-important in setting goals is to consider the value system you choose to live by. If money or material objects are your highest values, the questions you ask *before* you set your goals will be: How much will it cost? How much money will I make? What are the fringe benefits?

If security is your chief value, you'll ask these questions before you set your goals: Can I be sure of success? Is it risky? Is there a possibility of failure?

If Christ's Spirit lives within you, then you'll live by the *Service Value System*, which is placing enormous value on unselfishly serving your fellow man, and the first questions you'll raise in your goal setting will be: Will this help people who are hurting? Will this make me into a more beautiful person? Will this bring the best out of me—or the worst? Will this be a chance to prove my faith in a big God?

Man may not always make his goals, but his goals will always make the man.

———◆———

If You Fail to Plan,
You Are Planning to Fail

Set definite goals. Write them out. Draw a picture. Imprint them into your subconscious through the video channel of your eye. Now affirm positively, *out loud*, your hope for achievement. Visualize, then verbalize your goals. In so doing you are conditioning your subconscious through the audio as well as the video input channel of your body and mind. Repeat this mind-conditioning treatment daily and you will be instructing your subconscious to direct your life toward the realization of determined goals. Set a timetable to accomplish each phase, to create the pressure upon yourself to begin, and continue to progress steadily toward your goal. It is important that you set a definite time limit by which each phase must be accomplished. Otherwise, procrastination and delay will pilot your project, and with such commanders your goal may never be reached.

Ask yourself: What would be a great thing to do with my life before I die? Whatever it is, decide to do it! If it's more education you need, get it! If it's more money you need, find it! It's out there waiting to be invested in exciting new projects, plans, and people! If it's more talent you need, determine to acquire the skill—or hire the talent. Whatever you do—don't blow the opportunities that are still before you. God is desperately trying to instill a dream into your imagination. Don't torpedo it by saying it's impossible.

—◆—

Always Have a New Goal

Your greatest danger will not be failure to reach your goal; the greatest danger is that you'll make it and stop growing. Understand that goal setting is a never-ending activity of living persons and institutions. It is the pulse beat that tells you there's life here. "I hope you live to see all your dreams come true, Dr. Schuller," someone said to me. I objected. "I hope I don't! Or I will have died before I die physically. When a man has reached his goals and fails to set new goals, he's stopped living and is merely existing. A man dies when he stops dreaming. Fear not that you shall die. Fear rather that you shall stop living before you die!"

This is a universal life principle: when an organism, an individual, or an institution stops growing, the seeds of decline, decay, and death are planted. Make your goals large enough or expandable enough so you will not be boxed in when you reach them. Otherwise you will start failing just when you have started succeeding. Remember the principle taught by A. N. Whitehead, the great English philosopher: "Most great dreams of great dreamers are not fulfilled: They're transcended." So get exciting goals and come alive!

Not having a goal is more to be feared than not reaching a goal.

—◆—

Don't Stop at the Top!

Once you have reached the mountaintop, don't stop! Until every hungry person in the world is fed; every crying person is comforted; every depressed person has cause to smile again; every discouraged person is encouraged; and every lethargic person is motivated—don't stop possibilitizing.

"To whom much is given, from him much will be required," Jesus taught (Luke 12:48). Success carries with it a wonderfully heavy responsibility to use this new power as a lever to shift the world a little closer to God! Now is the time not to luxuriate, vegetate, or procrastinate, but to dedicate!

Now you have a power base. Use it! Now you have influence. Wield it! Now you have success. Share it! On the peak catch a peek— a new vision, a new dream, a loftier goal! Don't stop at the top!

Lord,
Thank you for great goals!
Let them be my uplifting aims.
But never let my targets become ceilings!
Amen.

—◆—

Nest, Don't Roost

You may be tempted to retire, relax, and spend the rest of your time enjoying your victory and accomplishment. You resist the thought of running into any more of those daring, fearful ventures. But you are to *nest* on the crest, not *roost!* Roosting is sleeping, getting fat, and saying, "I have success," "I have fortune," "I received the promotion," "I have my degree," or "I landed the job." Nesting is hatching out ideas for greater means of serving people. That feeds your self-esteem. And self-esteem will not last long. It will grow stale. You cannot live on yesterday's laurels or yesterday's awards. Fame is fleeting. Fortunes can be quickly dissipated, or threatened through the shifting sands of uncertain and unstable financial developments, nationally and internationally as well as privately. The only safe way to continue to meet your legitimate ego needs is to offer yourself as a channel for good.

And that means *looking beyond!*

—◇—

Don't Look Back

God alone knows how many good books have been burned, how many inspiring ideas have been cast into the wastebasket, how many great projects, programs, and marriages have been discarded by their creators who quit just before the miracle was about to happen.

There come times in the lives of most people when it seems utterly crazy to keep going. . . . I found hanging-on power in words that I had learned years before from my grandfather.

He was an immigrant from the Netherlands who pioneered in the unspoiled Iowa plains. In this land of the Sioux Indians he bought a plow and broke the virgin prairie. The trick, of course, was to plow a straight furrow when there were no boundaries. Here's how he did it.

He walked to the top of the hill, drove a stake. On the stake he tied a red handkerchief. He walked back down the hill and jabbed the sharp tip of the plow into the grass-covered prairie, fixed his eye on the red flag waving in the wind, and whipped his horses with a loud "Haaaigh!" That's how he plowed his first furrow. "Never take your eye off the flag," he used to tell the late-arriving pioneers. "Once you have hit dirt, and have started for the flag, don't look back. You may slip, you may stumble, you may get tired, and you may have to sit down, but whatever you do, *don't look back or you will plow a crooked furrow.*"

Then my grandfather liked to quote the powerful Bible verse: "No man having put his hand to the plow and looking back is fit for the kingdom of God." Don't look back. Don't accept failure. Don't accept defeat.

———◇———

Don't Surrender to Fear

The Bible says, "God has not given us a spirit of fear, but of power and of love and of a sound mind" (2 Tim. 1:7). That means when you surrender to fears, you can be sure the fears did not come from God. God does not give us the spirit of fear. God gives us the spirit of power and love and a sound mind.

If you have many fears, all you have to do is cure yourself of one fear, and that's the fear of failure. This will help: "I'd rather attempt something great and fail than attempt nothing and succeed."

I admire people who make a commitment and stick their neck out. I admire a person who tries to reach the top and doesn't make it. Perhaps he is someone who declares his candidacy for public office in a sincere desire to be a public servant for community good. He can be sure that he will be criticized and condemned, and probably misinterpreted and distorted. His ego will surely take an awful beating. What does he get out of it? Even if he loses the race, he is a winner because he has conquered his fear of trying. In doing so, he has won his biggest battle. Every loser who tries to do something great is really a winner.

—◆—

Face Your Fears

Strip away the masks, burn the costumes, tear down the facades, discover the real, root emotion. Behind the excuses, laziness, practicality, realism, and other guises of negative thinking is—*fear*.

People are negative because they are afraid. They are afraid of being disappointed. Call it the fear of dashed hopes. Call it the fear of having your dreams turn to ashes. Call it the fear of failure.

"I don't want to be disappointed. So I don't think I'll try." That's negative thinking. That's fearful thinking.

Now if you could learn how to deal with disappointments, if you could learn to lose without being defeated, would you dare to think positively?

If you will learn how to be disappointed without being discouraged, you need never be defeated. You'll never experience final failure. You will set higher goals. You will try again. When you realize that the worst that can happen is that you may have to face a disappointment, then you will be transformed from a doubter to a believer, from a negative thinker to a positive thinker.

———◇———

Reject Fear

No force, no emotion is more paralyzing than fear. It stops a sales-person about to make a call; the young man about to propose mar-riage; a job hunter about to seek an interview; an executive moments before making a decisive move; a seeker after truth about to commit his life to God.

In the whole sordid, sorry spectacle of human fears, none is more destructive and defeating than the fear of failure. Reject fear as the controlling force of your life. Discard such negative thinking as *flawed thinking!*

Some of you have lived your whole lives in fear. You have been taught to be skeptical and suspicious. You believe it is prudent to be cautious. In the process you may actually have become addicted to a deeply rooted, pessimistic mental outlook.

—◈—

Suffocate Your Fears

Isolate yourself from those who would tell you, "It can't be done,"
"It'll never work," "Somebody else tried it and failed," "It's never
been done before."

Isolate yourself from such destructive, negative forces. Isolate
yourself against the persons who generate depressing, discouraging vibrations. Suffocate your fears. Deprive them of their life
support systems.

---◆---

A Prayer for Confidence

It is flowing into me now, for my conscience is clear.
I have made the right decision.
I am not afraid of problems.
I will face challenges calmly and serenely
for God is behind me. He will help me.
If I must go through difficult times, he will rescue me.
I feel his spirit of confidence surging in my heart now.
With him I cannot possibly fail.
"If God is for me who can be against me?"
I have a strong feeling that everything
is going to work out just beautifully.
Thank you, God.
Amen.

---◆---

Fear Not

Make your fears work for you—not against you.

"I couldn't possibly live without the unknown in front of me," says Pierre Boulez, music director of the New York Philharmonic. This emotion you tend to call fear will be relabeled "mysteries of the future." So you begin to turn your fears into a positive force to motivate you:

Fear not that you might fail. . . . *Fear rather* that you will never succeed.

Fear not that you might be hurt. . . . *Fear rather* that you might never grow.

Fear not that you might love and lose. . . . *Fear rather* that you might never love at all.

Fear not that people might laugh at your mistakes. . . . *Fear rather* that God will address you "O you of little faith."

Fear not that you might fail again. . . . *Fear rather* that you might have made it if you had dared to try again.

Ready? Up with the big idea. Get set to start. Risky? Good! It's your chance to live in the dimension of faith. Oscar Wilde said, "An idea that isn't dangerous is hardly worth calling an idea."

My friend Fred Jarvis writes simple lines, but they are telling! "'Tis not your failure but low aim that is the crime and awful shame. Aim right. Aim high and raise your goal. With God plan big. With God plan bold."

—◆—

Courage from Faith

The Bible is filled with commands to be courageous. Someone counted the "fear nots" in the Bible and discovered that there are 365 verses with this divine command—one for every day of the year! Verses such as:

- "Fear not. . . . When you pass through the waters . . . they shall not overflow you. When you walk through the fire, you shall not be burned. . . . For I am the LORD your God. I will be with you" (Isa. 43:1–3).

- "Be strong and of good courage; do not be afraid, nor be dismayed, for the LORD your God is with you wherever you go" (Josh. 1:9).

- "For God has not given us a spirit of fear, but of power and of love and of a sound mind" (2 Tim. 1:7).

- "If you have faith as a mustard seed you will say to this mountain, 'Move from here to there,' and it will move; and nothing will be impossible for you" (Matt. 17:20).

. . . Observe now how *faith is the force that sets you free to succeed.*

—◆—

Never Fear Again

Join the N.F.A. Club. That's the Never Fear Again Club. How do you get in this club? Develop a strong personal faith in God. The deeply religious person is unflappable. A distinguished, elderly gentleman of my acquaintance puts it this way: "The Man who watches over me never makes any mistakes."

A student who is taking a most challenging college course tells me he writes his fears on a piece of paper, wraps them in a circle, and pierces the paper with an arrow that represents Jesus Christ.

One of the boldest of American businessmen was the late Robert LeTourneau. He shared the secret of his daring in this simple thought: "God is my partner. How could you ever be afraid if you had a partner like that?"

"Every time I go before the cameras, or walk on stage, I pray, 'Use me, Lord, use me,'" my friend Doris Day told me. She added, "There's always the danger in my business that one personalizes his work. When I came to see myself as a channel for God to use, I stopped worrying about possible goofs I might make."

Show me a person with a consuming dream coupled with a deep unshakable faith and I'll show you a champion mountain-mover. He's positive he'll succeed. He believes the Bible verse "In everything you do put God first and He will crown your efforts with success" (Prov. 3:6).

Ethel Waters has this slogan: "God don't sponsor no flops."

—◆—

Blinded to the Real World

There was a time when my children were little that I was going through some torturing times with the development of my church. I had colossal burdens and pressures. And although I was going through the motions of being a pastor, a husband, and a father, my heart was not really in any of these. It was blocked by despair, depression, and fear. . . .

It was not until I cried out to God and asked Him to release me from my anxieties and worries that I was able once more to feel His presence. Like a finger pressing into my brain, He touched me, and I felt the fear and the despair drain out of me. In its place flowed peace, joy, and hope, despite the obstacles that still lay ahead.

When God touched me, my ears were opened. I could once again hear what my family was saying to me. My eyes were opened. I could once again see the beauty that God had created. I could even see possible solutions for the overwhelming problems I was facing.

Worry, anxiety, pressures, frustrations—all of these can cause us to be blinded to the real world all around us. When we take this one step further, you can see how easy it would be for some emotional blockage to keep us from being aware of the presence of God.

"Blessed are the pure in heart, for they shall see God." I believe Jesus is teaching that if we have emotional and spiritual health we will be able to "see" God, to believe in Him.

—◇—

Unlock Your Negative Thinking

I talked to a businessman who said, "I've failed, but it's not my fault." And do you know why he said that? Because he blamed his failure on everybody else. He attacked the unions, government regulations, the tax structure, and the competition. I had to say to him, in as friendly and yet as firm a manner as I could, "Sir, in the final analysis you threw in the towel, they didn't. You said, 'I give up.' You decided to quit." At that point he finally admitted, "I guess I did."

If you fail it is because you choose to fail. And there are reasons why many people choose to fail. The price is too high. Total commitment is too costly (you'll eliminate all other options and alternatives if you're totally committed), so the risk is too great. Your security or your freedom is threatened by total commitment. Remember, associates, family, friends, or enemies may create problems for you, but nobody but you can and will ever make the final decision to quit. And nobody has failed until he's decided to throw in the towel. Only you can choose to kill your dream. Nobody else can make that decision.

You must believe in success. After all, the alternative is to believe in failure. And God has not planned your life to be a failure. For when you fail, many other innocent persons will be hurt. So, to accept failure is the ultimate selfish act.

Believe in success, for success means discovering God's beautiful plan for your life and allowing it to develop to its fullest potential.

God plans for success and believes in it! Get with it!

Real Failure

"So what's real failure?" you ask yourself at this point. The answer comes clear. Real failure is to fail as a person. To yield to cowardice in the face of an urgent but risky venture. To fearfully retreat from a high call to noble duty because you can see the possibility of imperfection in your performance of that duty.

To be more concerned about protecting your pride from an embarrassing failure than about promoting a wonderful and worthy cause. To demote faith from the leadership of your future life and promote fear to a power-base position of authority over your destiny. This is real failure as a person.

Failure is no disgrace. "Not failure but a low aim is a crime." At least you had the courage to try. It is more honorable to try something worthwhile and fail than never to attempt any worthy venture. Play-it-safe people seldom win the applause and the respect of others—they never do anything to merit congratulations!

—◆—

The Fear of Failure

Failure doesn't mean you are a failure. . . . *It does mean* you haven't succeeded yet.

Failure doesn't mean you have accomplished nothing. . . . *It does mean* you have learned something.

Failure doesn't mean you have been a fool. . . . *It does mean* you had a lot of faith.

Failure doesn't mean you've been disgraced. . . . *It does mean* you were willing to try.

Failure doesn't mean you don't have it. . . . *It does mean* you have to do something in a different way.

Failure doesn't mean you are inferior. . . . *It does mean* you are not perfect.

Failure doesn't mean you've wasted your life. . . . *It does mean* you have a reason to start afresh.

Failure doesn't mean you should give up. . . . *It does mean* you must try harder.

Failure doesn't mean you'll never make it. . . . *It does mean* it will take a little longer.

Failure doesn't mean God has abandoned you. . . . *It does mean* God has a better idea!

A Life of Regrets

Suppose you have a great idea, but having surrendered to fear of failure, you let the golden opportunity pass you by. You remain safe from fear of embarrassment but now you are bored. *Boredom doesn't build self-esteem.* What does boredom do? It gives you loads of time to think, "It might have worked."

To quote John Greenleaf Whittier:

For of all sad words of tongue or pen,
The saddest are these: "It might have been."

You grow old, collecting and nursing a multitude of regrets. Why didn't I do this? Why didn't I do that? Why didn't I buy it when I had a chance? To further depress yourself, you may see someone else seizing the same opportunity. They are successful and you become jealous. The pangs of further jealousy will make you more bitter and inspire further negative thoughts and actions. Thus fear of failure does not protect your self-respect—it prevents and aborts it. If you heed your fears you'll die never knowing what a great person you might have been.

—◆—

Exposed

Perfectionism, also, is a fear of rejection. You fear that failure will expose you as an imperfect person. Think realistically—and realize no one is perfect. And no intelligent person expects you to be perfect. Beautiful and good people will never reject you when your imperfection is exposed by failure. It may just prove that you're a human being. Every individual is a failure in some way, at some time, on some level. Remember: "To err is human, to forgive is divine."

In the final analysis people will accept or reject you not for what you do—but for what kind of person you are.

Better to do something imperfectly than to do nothing perfectly!

◆

Don't Get Trapped
by Perfectionism

The positive ideas that flow into your brain come from God. Don't reject the ideas simply because of your awareness of your own imperfections. Perfectionism keeps many people from ever embracing the kind of faith that could mature into a mountain-moving force.

An often-told folk tale illustrates the futility of perfectionism: A man found a beautiful pearl with one tiny flaw. He thought if he could remove that tiny imperfection, the pearl would be the world's most priceless. So he peeled off the first layer. But the flaw was still there. He took off the next layer, thinking the flaw would surely be removed, but it remained. He continued to take off layer after layer, until, finally, the flaw was gone—but so was the pearl!

Of course, no idea is perfect. No idea is without its built-in problems. But trust that the positive potential in an idea is powerful enough to merit your continued support.

—◆—

What a Friend!

You have never failed, Lord,
to be my one, essential, intimate friend.
When I was:
Lonely in striving—you encouraged me.
Lonely in struggling—you lifted me.
Lonely in serving—you supported me.
Lonely in suffering—you comforted me.
Lonely in sinning—you forgave me.
Lonely in sinking—you renewed me.
Lonely in succeeding—you rejoiced with me.
What a friend I have in Jesus!
Thank you, Lord.
Amen.

—◇—

Faith: The Key to Reality

What is so sensational about a positive faith in a caring and compassionate God is the honesty of it all! Believers are not Pollyanna people. Faith is reality thinking. It says, "Hey! I'm going to walk through the valley of the shadow of death."

Secular people don't want to talk about the subject. They don't even want to think about the cemeteries. Historic believers are the reality thinkers. We know we will all go through the valley of the shadow of death. We are ready for it.

The Psalmist was the super reality thinker. "Yes, though I [whatever my age] *walk* through the valley of the shadow of death, I will fear no evil." Just think of those words—not crawl, not creep, not cringe, but *walk* upright.

Walk. "Yes, though I walk *through* the valley." *Through*, not to or into, but *through* it. God doesn't send us *to* the valley, He walks with us *through* the valley. This is part of the process of living, and death is no problem as long as you are not afraid. The Psalmist was not afraid.

"Yes, though I walk through the valley of the *shadow* of death." To the Psalmist, death was just a *shadow*, not the real thing. He did not deny the reality that a human being goes through the experience called death, but death is never really real to us who are believers. It is a transition, the process we go through to enter eternal life.

Shadow? Guess what? That is a positive word because if you see a *shadow*, you can be sure there is a sun! Or a bright light! There is a light behind every *shadow*.

———◆———

Leave It to Me

I believe that our greatest temptation is a failure to learn the wisdom of taking "the longer look."

Timing. Is it stressful without faith? You bet it is! But real faith is a force far more powerful than stress.

Do you feel the weight of timing? Let me help you with those pressures.

Don't ever drop the curtain on tomorrow! God's delays aren't God's denials. No, God answers every prayer. I've often said . . .

If the request isn't right, His answer is *no*.

If the timing isn't right, His answer is *slow*.

If you aren't ready—yet—His answer is *grow*.

When everything's right and ready, His answer is *go!*

I was facing a real challenge in my ministry. I had invested more time and more money into a project that wasn't working out as I planned and hoped. I prayed and then heard one sentence clearly in my mind: "Leave it to Me." It was one of the greatest gifts God had ever given me. I was able to turn it over to God and experience total, complete, beautiful peace of mind.

———◇———

Time to Reconnect

So important is timing in the architecture of successful living that one of the Ten Commandments deals with time management: "Remember the Sabbath to keep it holy" (Exod. 20:8). Tradition carries on this truth learned from experience by preceding generations. One day in seven, you should plan to *retreat, relax,* and *regroup* as a family. Review, reload, and prepare for reentry on Monday morning. Reconnect with God and faith.

Take time to fill your spiritual fuel tank with gas. Tomorrow is Monday. You don't want to take off on an empty tank. Remember?

I'm convinced that people who discipline themselves to take one day a week to refuel their emotional gas tank will keep their energy up. Stop on Sunday to recharge your positive mental attitude in your place of positive meditation. God sends creative ideas into minds that open up in quiet prayer and meditation, letting the subconscious know it's protected from uninvited, pressure-producing interruptions.

Are Your Plans Delayed?

The timing may be delayed. And we must be emotionally prepared to put a positive spin on that!

So stop and pray. Time out! Check your connections with God. Is this new venture why you were born? Is this daring dream God's purpose for your life? Yes, the price in success will include expenditures of time and effort as well as money. But don't be surprised to look back and see that the toughest problem was "waiting for the moment."

Dealing with delays? You did it! You didn't quit, walk away, throw in the towel. Timing—it's everything!

So plan to stay. Hang in there!

Just never, never, never quit! If you quit, you'll be abandoning the base you've built, and then what? You'll never be satisfied, pleased, or content if you quit doing and being what started out as real pleasure. *Welcome* delays. They may be God's gifts of grace, increasing your chances of eventual *success with a smile.*

Look back! See how many good things have happened to you since you were born. Add up all your accomplishments from all your yesterdays, and you'll be surprised to see you've come from nowhere to somewhere.

Look around! See how many good things are happening to you today.

Look ahead! Imagine how many good things can happen in all of your tomorrows—if you'll only keep the faith!

—◆—

God's Timing—or Ours?

Are we moving too fast? Or are we moving too slowly? Should we plunge ahead—or wait? What decision maker, facing opportunities, has not raised this question? For timing is all-important in every venture of life. If God is your partner, He will help you time things wisely.

Chances are God will time things out in such a way that when He answers your prayer, He will be answering many prayers. God is big. So big that when He answers one prayer, He answers many prayers. . . .

Be patient; God is working everything out. At the right time and in the right way everything will evolve beautifully.

> *Don't try to rush God.*
> *Mountains don't move overnight.*
> *Give God time to work His miracles.*
> *I have seen God dissolve resentments,*
>   *resolve frustrations,*
>   *fill lonely hearts with new love,*
>   *and wash away hurts like a new wave*
>   *washes away scars on sand*
>   *scratched by children's sticks.*
> *God can get you out of a rut,*
>   *onto a new road,*
>   *and over the mountain that seemed impassable,*
>   *if you will be patient.*

Stop Making Excuses for Not Starting!

Procrastination is your greatest enemy. Delays will turn pregnant opportunities into hollow possibilities. If you don't have the faith to move ahead *now*, don't be surprised when that bigger believer appears and launches your idea successfully. You'll moan and groan saying, "I thought about doing that—why didn't I?"

Goethe wrote: "Lose this day loitering, twill be the same story tomorrow and the next more dilatory. Indecision brings its own delays and days are lost lamenting over lost days. Action—there is courage, magic in it. Anything you can do, or think you can, begin it. Once started, the mind grows heated. Begin the job and the work will be completed."

What's holding you back?

◆

Start on Time—Now!

Someone once said to me, "Life is too short to do what we want to do." I answered, "Oh no it's not—not if you start on time!"

Wake up! Come alive! Snap the cords of laziness! Break the chains of lethargy! "It is high time to awake out of sleep" (Rom. 13:11). "Truly, *now* is the right time—*now* is the day of salvation" (2 Cor. 6:2). "This is the day" (Ps. 118:24).

Make up your mind to *act now!* Escape from the prison of inertia! *Do it now!* Take some action *now*—telephone, write a letter, do something! Move! Act! Start! Begin! Get Going! *Now!*

Shake up the negative thoughts. Shake all impossibility thoughts out of your mind! Shake them out! "Quit you like men—be strong" (1 Cor. 16:13).

Break up the obstacles. Shatter the barriers. You can. It's like making a doorway in the great wall of China. How? Remove one stone at a time. Break your biggest problems into small, workable pieces.

Take up the crowning accomplishment that is your destiny! You'll walk away with honors. People will respect and admire you. God will bless you. How happy you will be! You'll become the person you always wanted to be. Start acting like a Possibility Thinker—*now!*

Ready, Set . . .

Think "Begin!" Don't let your *possibilities* be suffocated by procrastination. Go! Now!

You want to wait till the "hurt" is all gone?

You want to wait until you have answers to every question?

You want to wait until you're sure you won't be "hurt" again and put "out" again next time the way you were last time?

You'll start when you can be sure you'll never fail?

You'll take the first step only when you can be sure you can complete the journey?

You'll make the first move when you've got the burst of inspiration?

Come on! Grow up! Enough mourning and moaning is enough!

◆

Deciding to Begin

At every age you need a new *peak* experience to give you a *peek* experience, a new vision of what you can be and a new consciousness of what you can do. You envision that what you can be far exceeds anything you've ever been before. . . .

How can you have a peak experience?

You can begin by dreaming a greater dream. The dream gives rise to desire, the desire gives rise to the daring-to-do, the daring-to-do gives rise to the deciding-to-begin, and the deciding-to-begin gives rise to the deciding-to-try *seriously*.

Some of you may be afraid to begin. You don't think you can finish. You think, "Can I make it all the way to the top?"

Here's a great concept: decide to begin and then decide to keep going. Don't worry about the top. Just decide to start and *keep going until you are past the point of no return.*

For ten years I have been a confirmed, dedicated, practicing jogger. One day, as I prepared to run, I realized I wasn't in the mood for running my customary four miles. My home is six miles from my office, so I got into my running suit and decided, "I'm only going to run just a little more than halfway from the house to the office." When I was a little more than halfway from the house to the office, what could I do? *It would then be easier to finish than to turn back.* In that way I finished a six-mile run.

I use this technique a lot in my life. When I know there is something that I should do but can't get up the drive, I only make the commitment to go as far as the point of no return. Then I'm trapped and I have to complete the job. The key is in deciding to begin.

—◇—

Intentional Urgency

Build a sense of urgency into your thinking and get going! "Winter is coming." "A test is coming up." "Relatives are coming to visit." "I'll soon be too old to go." "The inspector will be dropping around." "The boss will be calling for a report." "I'll have to step on the scale in the doctor's office next month."

Average people produce under pressures generated by events, circumstances, or other persons who control their life in part or in whole. Exceptional persons produce under urgent pressures they have deliberately generated themselves!

So they first sign a contract to deliver by a certain date; then they release a public announcement of their intention to produce. So they commit themselves in such a way that they have to go ahead with it! . . .

Schedule planning sessions, decision-making meetings, and problem-solving meetings. Write them on your personal calendar. By doing this you ensure your future time. You will succeed if you will only make time to work your plan. Remind yourself that you will certainly fail if you do not block out the time. Nothing will happen unless you mark it on your calendar *now!*

Now break up your dream into time stages. Mark on your calendar the beginning and the concluding date of the planning stage, the launching stage, the problem-solving stages, and the celebration of success date! Aim at a "special" day like Christmas or New Year's or your next birthday. Then promise yourself a reward on that day. A new suit of clothes, a trip, a special dinner in your favorite restaurant. Now tell yourself, "I've got a great thing going—I must not stop it!"

————◇————

Selfish Pride

Why is it so hard for us to ask for help? Is it because we don't want to admit we lack knowledge? Or are we afraid of being turned down, put down, or torn down? Why do people dare to set big goals? Are there people who are afraid of thinking big, talking big, or trying big? The humble people? Selfish pride leads to ruin. The person who never thinks big, talks big, or tries big isn't being humble. He is probably so proud that he is simply not going to risk failure by thinking big, talking big, and trying big. That's how selfish pride leads to failure!

If pride prevents you from succeeding, you are very selfishly going to prevent yourself from being the helpful person you could be. Then failure becomes doubly selfish!

By contrast, sacrificial pride is the strong self-confidence that believes it can succeed and dares to sacrifice its arrogance on the altar of some noble attempt, unashamedly calling out for all the help it can attract along the way.

—◇—

Faith

Lord, I believe
in the sun, even when it is behind the clouds;
in the seed, even when it lies unsprouted under the ground;
in faith, even when I have been betrayed;
in love, even when I have been rejected;
in hope, even when I have been hurt;
in God, even when you do not answer my prayers.
Amen.

---◆---

When God Answers "No"

Someone said God answers every prayer in these words: "I love you." Because He loves you He answers every prayer in one of four ways.

When the conditions are not right, God says, "No." Actually, He is even then giving you what you really want because what you really want is what is best for you. . . .

In the 1920s, a young minister, Oswald Smith, wanted above all else to become a missionary in another country. He prayed, "God, I want to be a missionary . . . open the door for me."

That was a true prayer. It was not begging, it was not selfish, it was a prayer in which a human soul was trying to become the person God wanted him to be. When Dr. Smith stood before the examining board for the approval of foreign missionaries, he failed the test. He didn't meet their qualifications.

In spite of his efforts, the doors to overseas ministries were shut. One of his reactions to this was to wonder if prayer really works. Here he was offering his life to God and God's answer was clearly no. Then a brilliant idea came to his mind. "If I can't go, I'll build a church to send others out there." He did. No pastor has ever established a church that has even come close to accomplishing what Oswald Smith's Peoples Church has. In the span of history, we can see how beautifully God answered the desire of Dr. Smith's prayer even when He said no to his precise request. God said no, for God had a bigger and better idea.

—◆—

When God Answers "Slow"

When the time is not right, God says, "Slow." Nowhere in the entire Bible can you find a Bible verse that says that God will do anything you ask Him to do when you snap your fingers. God does not offer an instamatic prayer-answering service.

God maintains control in the area of the *why* and the *when*. If God answers no to your very sincere prayer, and you ask Him why, God will not answer or explain. God doesn't answer your why question because raising the question means you are not satisfied with the no.

You want to argue and God refuses to be drawn into an argument. He knows that any explanation He might give would not satisfy you.

If God answered every prayer at the snap of your fingers He would become your servant—not your master. God would be working for you instead of you working for God.

God's delays are not God's denials. God's timing is perfect. Patience is needed in prayer. Some people don't suffer from doubt as much as from impatience.

A man said to me, "I have lost faith in prayer." After listening to him I said, "You have not really lost faith in prayer because you are still praying. You haven't lost faith. You simply lost patience."

Longtime members of our church know that we spell the word "faith" . . . P-A-T-I-E-N-C-E.

"O rest in the Lord, wait patiently for Him and He shall give thee thy heart's desire. O rest in the Lord, wait patiently, wait patiently for Him."

---◆---

When God Answers "Grow"

When you are not right God answers, "Grow." God answers prayers when people are ready for it. The ambitious person who doesn't rise to the top immediately often prays for success. God answers, "Grow." Power that comes too fast corrupts. If you are not ready, it will spoil you.

Do you have prayers that are not being answered? Maybe *you* have to grow. Do you face an unsolved problem? Perhaps there is something you have to do.

If your mind is infested with negative emotions, you'll be out of rhythm with the God of the universe and your prayer will not be effective. . . .

Is there an opportunity you have been working on and it does not seem to be working out? Perhaps you need to change!

—◆—

God Answers "Go!"

When everything is right God says, "Go!" Then miracles happen! Barriers tumble! Mountains are conquered! Problems disappear and heartaches dissolve!

A hopeless alcoholic is set free! A drug addict is cured! A doubter becomes as a child in his belief! Diseased tissue responds to treatment, and healing begins!

The door to your dream suddenly swings open, and there stands God saying, "Go!" . . .

Try praying big, honest, clean, affirmative prayers, and you'll become the person God wants you to be!

> *Thank you, Lord, for bringing me to the place*
> *where love can knock at the door of my heart.*
> *O Father, do not let me be afraid.*
> *I shall not resist your affectionate touch.*
> *Let me, O Lord, have the spirit of a little child*
> *and dare to respond and run with open arms to*
> *your call of love.*
> *Amen.*

God's Plan

"And whatever you ask in prayer, you will receive it if you have faith" (Matt. 21:22). Does this mean that God will give anyone anything he asks for? Of course not. We often don't have the wisdom to know what's best for us.

In a small community in Germany I heard this legend. "Years ago we were troubled with poor harvests. So the villagers prayed, 'Lord, for one year promise us that you will give us exactly what we ask for—sun and rain, when we ask for it.'" According to the legend, God agreed. When villagers called for rain, He sent rain. When they called for sun, He sent sun. Never did the corn grow taller, or the wheat so thick as it did that season. As the harvest time approached, joy turned to sadness when the farmers saw to their shock and dismay that the cornstalks had no corn, the wheat stalks produced no grain, and the leafy fruited trees bore no fruit. "O God!" the simple people prayed. "You have failed us." And God replied, "Not so my children. I gave you all that you asked for."

"Then why, Lord," they cried, "have we no fruit or kernel or grain?"

"Because," God answered, "you did not ask for the harsh north wind." Without the winds, of course, there was no pollination. . . .

Jesus did not say that God answers all selfish begging, childish and pitiful pleading. Jesus did say that God answers all prayer. People often pray for utterly materialistic and selfish things. When they receive no miraculous answer to these requests to a deity, they, in doubt and cynicism, say, "See, prayer does not work!" They called it prayer, but God did not call it prayer.

Cast Your Net on the Other Side

In Scripture we learn how one afternoon, as Jesus spoke from the shore of Lake Gennesaret, great crowds pressed in on Him to hear His message. He noticed Peter and another fisherman washing their nets nearby. Stepping into an empty boat, Jesus asked Peter to push out into the water so He could address the crowds. When He had finished speaking, Jesus turned to Peter and said, "Now go out where it is deeper, cast your nets, and catch some fish."

"Master," Peter replied, "we have toiled all night and caught nothing" (Luke 5:5).

For Peter, a most competent fisherman, to fish all night and catch nothing is like Beverly Sills not hitting a high note. It's Arnold Palmer not shooting par. It's Norman Vincent Peale, that great positive thinker, saying, "I can't do it! It won't work!"

Peter had toiled all night with no results whatsoever. And then Jesus recommended that he start over again!?

When you've toiled all night and caught nothing, what do you do? You use Possibility Thinking. *Never, never cash in, but cast in on the other side.*

When Peter heard Jesus' next words, he was incredulous. "Launch out into the deep and let down your nets for a catch." No doubt Peter was tired and Jesus' advice seemed preposterous, but Peter did as he was told. Suddenly, he felt the glorious weight of fish in his net, so many fish that the net began to tear as he struggled to lift it into the boat.

—◇—

Don't Be Afraid to Start Over

When you are faced with having to start over again, it is tempting to become cynical. Perhaps you want to quit school because you don't know where it is leading you. Maybe you want to give up writing because all you ever get are rejection slips. You may want to withdraw from relationships because people have treated you shabbily. Perhaps you have even tried to find assurance and joy in religion, but it, too, has come up like an empty net.

If you are tempted to look at life in terms of cynicism and futility, my friend, I want to show you how Possibility Thinking can help you find love and joy! Here's how to find self-fulfillment: First, look out for your worst enemy—yourself. Second, listen to advice from positive-thinking people. Third, lower your net again. Try, and keep trying, until you make your catch.

—◆—

Hope for a Breakthrough

If you are at the bottom, weighed down by overwhelming circumstances, if you are at the edge of panic, the most dangerous thing you can do is to make a negative, irreversible decision.

Keep believing, and there will be a breakthrough. You *will* break through the challenges that you are currently facing. You *will* break through the defeats that have set you back. You *will* emerge on the other side and say, *"It was all for the better!"*

The first question you will probably ask is: *When will a breakthrough happen?* It could happen today, tomorrow, or the next day. I don't know when, and neither can you. God alone knows the answer to that question.

The next question you may ask is: *How long can I hold on?* A lot longer than you think you can!

Every psychiatrist will say it: "We see patients, month after month, year after year. Suddenly one day, through nothing specific that we could tell that we did, the skin that drooped and was gray becomes pink; the eye that was dull gets a sparkle! It's a phenomenal moment. For hope is a phenomenon! We don't know what triggers the birth of hope or where it comes from. We don't think it comes from us. What we do know is what happens in the person! When a person finds hope, there is total renewal."

You can find new hope when you realize that today is the *beginning! What looks like an end never is unless you decide to make it the end.*

God isn't finished with you yet. Just give Him a chance to show there is a breakthrough for you.

Keep Growing, Keep Reaching

If you think you can marry, have children, get a good job, save a little money, plan for retirement, and then, at a nice age, wrap everything up to spend the rest of your days in the sunshine, you're being misled. Retirement may seem wonderful when you look ahead, but it won't be when it arrives. You'll soon find out how quickly emptiness sets in, because you just can't stop at the top!

There must be a meaningful struggle all your life or you will die before your time! You start dying when you stop struggling! Why does God give us victories after struggling? Not that we might stop and luxuriate or hibernate or vacillate or procrastinate, but that we might dedicate ourselves to conquering the new valley beyond that we never knew was there before. Don't stop at the top. Keep growing. Keep reaching. . . .

Stop eating and you die physically. Stop exercising and you die physically. Stop breathing and you die physically. Stop learning and you die intellectually. Stop praying and you die spiritually. Stop struggling and your self-esteem starts dying!

Die Climbing

There is an old cemetery in Switzerland where many of the great mountain climbers are buried. Some of the epitaphs are most appropriate, but there is one that stands out. One of the great mountain climbers died while trying to conquer a rugged peak many years ago. Three words are carved into the tombstone beneath his name: "He died climbing!" I love that! That's what God would like to put as the final sentence of your life and mine! "He didn't die luxuriating." "He didn't die hibernating." "He didn't die procrastinating." "He didn't die vegetating." "He *died climbing!*" The truth is if he hadn't died climbing, he would have been dead the moment he decided to stop climbing, for you can't stop at the top!

◆

Plenty of Time

A word of special warning to the senior citizen: don't underesti-
mate the time you still may have left! Following a Possibility
Thinking lecture on a Pacific cruise ship, an enthusiastic listener
told me, "I wish I had heard that thirty years ago. I could have
died a millionaire." I guessed his age at about fifty-seven. "How
old are you?" I asked. "Sixty-eight," he answered, smiling. "Then
you're not too old to begin!" I challenged. "You look so young and
healthy you just might live to be ninety-eight—that's thirty years
away! Start today, or twenty years from now you'll be moaning,
'Why didn't I start twenty years ago when I was still young?'"

   If you are so advanced in years that you cannot reasonably
imagine yourself living long enough to complete your dream,
then what? Consider not the time resources God has given you—
but consider the time resources God has! My dad planted a new
apple orchard when he was nearly eighty because he knew that
God would provide the time to bring the trees to full fruitfulness
for someone, someday, to enjoy!

How Old Are You?

General Douglas MacArthur, from the vantage point of his own ripe years, said in Los Angeles in 1956, "You are as young as your faith, as old as your doubt; as young as your confidence, as old as your fear; as young as your hope, as old as your despair. In the central place of every heart there is a recording chamber; so long as it receives messages of beauty, hope, cheer and courage, so long are we young. When the wires are all down and your heart is covered with the snows of pessimism and the ice of cynicism, then and then only are you grown old."

A man is not old until he has lost his vision. And a man is young as long as he sees possibilities around him!

God Is Able

Read these great "God is able" Bible verses and build faith to hold on to:

- "He is able to save completely all who come to God through Him" (Heb. 7:25, Living Translation).

- "He is able to help those who are tempted" (Heb. 2:18, RSV).

- "He is able to guard until that day what has been entrusted to me" (2 Tim. 1:12, RSV).

- "He is able to keep you from falling and slipping away" (Jude 2, Living Translation).

- "He is able to do far more abundantly than we ask or think" (Eph. 3:20, RSV).

—◇—

He Makes Me to Lie Down

[The Psalmist] openly admits that sometimes the shepherd forcibly takes the sheep from their field of play and food, and makes them lie down—"He makes me to lie down in green pastures." Which is his way of saying that trouble is not always trouble!

And what is trouble, you ask? You could get a variety of answers to that question.... Trouble is final exams when you haven't finished the textbook; or remembering today an important appointment you forgot yesterday; or finding yourself without a comb, hair disheveled, and important people waiting to see you; or trouble is running out of gas on a long lonely road at night in strange mountains. And trouble is many things far worse than any of these! Of course, there is such a thing as trouble!

But it is obvious that in our pitiful judgments we often label as troubles what in time and truth are really blessings in disguise. Mysteries of Providence we should call them.

I am indebted to a wonderful old Christian who was past ninety when confined to a bed. "I see you are having a little trouble," I sympathized. The smile wrinkles in her face cracked and she chided me, "Oh, no, I'm not having trouble. I just didn't know when to quit and the good Lord made me lie down. But I have been having a wonderful time reading His Word, and talking with Him at night when I couldn't sleep, and He turns this bed into a green pasture. 'He makes me to lie down in green pastures.'"

—◆—

God Slows Us Down

We all know that most of us adults in America are living too fast, too hard, and too strenuously. We are caught in a bumper-to-bumper way of living. We are always on the move—driving, going, just coming home, or just getting ready to go out—but always on the move, so that we hardly know how to relax for a quiet evening at home without taking something from a box or a bottle to unwind us. We are restless, nervous, fidgety. Even when we are relaxing, we have an almost guilty feeling that we should be doing something, or going somewhere!

All the while God is trying to say something: "Slow down and start living. Enjoy your friends, your family, and your faith!" But the voice of God is overpowered by the roar of the traffic on the freeway, the moan of ambulances, the wail of sirens, the growl of buses, the rude interruption of the doorbell. Jet airplanes, two-ton diesel trucks, trains, television, telephones fill our everyday world with noises the ears were never designed to tolerate. An irritating assortment of unnatural sounds drown out the silver-soft voice of God that whispers through the pines, and speaks through foaming waves that swish on salty sand. "Lie down, my child, and rest a while. Take a break from the freeway form of living. Your nerves weren't made to stand the strain, your body wasn't engineered for such stress, your eyes can't stand some of the temptations!"

—◇—

Trouble Is Not Always Trouble

But we refuse to lie down until God makes us lie down! And then, miserable victims of self-pity, we think that we are in trouble!

Oh, be slow to judge, my soul! Is it really trouble? Or is it a divinely disguised blessing? That sickness, that lost job, that unfaithful friend, that financial loss—be not swift to label it a wolf at the door. It may be a sheep in wolf's clothing!

Is the grinding wheel that puts a fresh edge on the knife, or the hoe that breaks up hard soil and plows out weeds, or the sharp knife of the gardener that prunes and snips useless growth to give greater strength to the roots and the trunk, or the north wind that forces the pine to send down roots of steel into granite earth, or the rod in the shepherd's hand that strikes the sheep lest it run blindly off a precipice, or the bloody surgeon's scalpel that cuts away the foreign tumor, or the sculptor's hard hammer and brutal chisel that chip and polish—are these not all our friends? The chisel, the hammer, the scalpel, the rod, the wind, the knife, the hoe, the wheel, are these not our friends?

Trouble is not always trouble! It is often God's way of making us lie down, turn around, sit still, pray, work harder, or start over again!

◆

When Is Trouble Not Trouble?

When is trouble not trouble, you ask? When it protects you from an unknown hazard on the road ahead, or shelters you from a sin that, unknown to you, lurks furtively in your path waiting to tempt and trip you, then trouble is not trouble!

When trouble cleans up collected clutter that you valued too highly and did not have the courage to discard or destroy, or when it tears out of your life an unworthy friend whom you were unable to help and who was not a good influence on your life, then trouble is not trouble!

When trouble makes you furious enough to fight for a good cause you were too busy to serve, or frustrates you so that you quit a job that was too long hiding your real talents and forces you to discover new skills and hidden talents that were lying undetected like veins of gold under cabbage fields, then trouble is not trouble!

When trouble causes two parties, long unspeaking, to bury the hatchet; when it makes a person forget himself and start thinking of others; when it makes a greedy man generous, a hard man compassionate, a cold heart warm, a thoughtless man considerate—then trouble is not without its reward!

When trouble teaches you valuable lessons that you would have been too blind to see, too arrogant to believe, or too stubborn to accept any other way than by this bed of pain; when it slams a door in your face to force you out of a rut that you would never have had the courage to leave and leads you down a new road through an open door, then trouble may be a most valuable experience!

OCTOBER 31

Trouble Changes Us

Trouble never leaves you where it found you. It either changes you into a *better* person or a *bitter* person. You have the freedom to choose what your problem will do to you. The weak time can become your peak time.

One cantankerous old man lived as if he was mad at the whole world. Then one day he had a stroke, which left him paralyzed. Years later, when an old friend paid him a visit, the former didn't seem to be the same person. The grouchy old man had become mellow. His roughness had become smooth and gentle. His eyes, which had been hard as steel, had become warm and soft. The worn, wrinkled face, once tight and stiff, was glowing with warmth. Noticing the transformation in the old man's personality, the friend said, "Sickness and trouble have a way of coloring the personality, don't they?" The elderly man looked up at him and replied in a quiet and gentle voice, "Yes, sickness has a way of coloring the personality, and I decided that I would pick the colors and make them beautiful!"

—◆—

Part of Life

Life's not fair. But is this what you deserve? It is imperative that you ask yourself this question and come up with a satisfactory answer, because it is the root of getting you successfully through any tragedy. It is also the foundation for building a new beginning.

The first question I hear from people when they get hurt is, "Why me?" But that's the wrong question. It can produce self-doubt and even self-contempt. The right question to ask is, Why not you? This question recognizes that *what happens to you is incidental to who you are.* Tragedies happen because tragedies are part of life. Death is part of life. You cannot have life without death, and you cannot have happiness without sadness. You cannot have life without hurts.

—◆—

When the Road Ahead Is Short

O God, from the vantage point of today the road ahead looks very short. I sense that I am about to reach the end.

Remind me that every time of ending is always a time of new beginning. Every time one door closes, another door opens. Every sunset is a move closer to a new sunrise. Death is always the prelude to resurrection.

Help me to forgive myself for my imperfections and faults. I dishonor you when I disgrace myself by nursing regrets over my human shortcomings. Help me to honor you by recalling great accomplishments you made possible through my life.

So let me come to the end of the road with pride behind me, love around me, and hope ahead of me—only to discover that what I thought was the end of the road is a bend in the road leading me into an exciting new world of opportunity or eternity. Amen.

---◈---

Try Changing Your Perspective

If life hasn't been fair to you, then maybe you need to fix your point of perspective. Perhaps you need to look at what you can do and learn to be more than you have ever been before. Perhaps you have been focusing on yourself too much. Perhaps you need to focus on others more. Perhaps you need to learn to work as a team with your spouse, with your children, with your boss.

It's never easy to change. It is often painful. But if life feels unfair to you, be fair to yourself. Ask yourself if life is trying to teach you something about yourself. More often than not we bring about our own pain. The good news is that we can change. It is never too late to learn and to grow. There are exciting new discoveries being made every day that can help us in our quest to be all that we are meant to be.

So if the picture of your life is askew, if things don't look right, start by fixing your perspective. Look at what you can work on. You'll be amazed at what you can do and be.

NOVEMBER 4

—◆—

Learn to Know God

Dear Jesus,
I've got to get to know You better. Please help me!
I can feel my spiritual and emotional walls crack.
I can hear old chains break.
I can feel my heart opening like a heavy old door
whose ancient seals have just begun to break.
I can sense the footsteps of Jesus walking into my life.
I am beginning to experience the joy of a soul that is being saved,
a life that is being born again.
Thank You, Lord! Life's not fair, but God is good.
Amen.

———◇———

Believe in Me

Be sure of this: God has designed human beings to be the one and only creature that differs from all animals by having the power to conceive of the possibility of an invisible, creative Higher Power we call God. This eternal and intelligent energy is constantly sending creative ideas into human minds. And if God can inspire me to believe it, He can help me to achieve it.

"What's the eternal, affectionate, redemptive Higher Power called God trying to tell me today?" I ask. And God answers, "Believe in me! Believe in the positive ideas I'm sending you! Believe in yourself—I do!" That's the message God is trying to get into all of our human heads and hearts today!

—◈—

What Will You Do with the Hurt?

God's purpose in creating humans was to create beings who could bring honor and glory to Him. Goodness isn't goodness unless it's a choice. Love isn't love unless it's a freely chosen option.

Here was the divine dilemma facing the Creator God: if He created such decision-making persons, then He, God, would take the ultimate risk in all creation. The risk was that these creatures called *persons* could choose to become selfish and sinful, capable of behavior marked by evil and injustice. This opened the door for hurt, rejection, and even death.

What is the answer to the ultimate question, Why does God permit and allow suffering? The answer is a mystery. But we do know that God permits humans to experience hurts, rather than exercising His paternalistic power and extinguishing the person-hood of human beings by removing their free will.

The *why?* remains wrapped in a mystery. The real question now begins with *what?* What is God doing about the sin? the suffering? the selfishness? the sickness? the death? What has He done? He has given all hurting human beings the freedom to choose to turn their crosses into crowns, their hurts into halos. With our free will intact, we can choose a reaction that turns torturous negative experiences into radiant positive ones that glorify and honor God!

So the final question is not a question you will ask God. The final question is one God will ask you: "What will you do—or what will *we* do together—with the hurt you face today?"

Now we turn reality thinking into Possibility Thinking.

◆

Compelled to Trust

Why? is the one question all innocent persons in pain cry out to the blackness that is deathly silent. *Why?* is the one question God is not obligated to answer. The truth is, when in our pain and hurt we call out "Why?" to God, we don't want an answer. We want out of the dark place. If God answered, He'd be drawn into an argument. His answer would only provoke more questions from us: "But why *me!?* I don't deserve it."

Why? is the normal, understandable, proper, legitimate question, but that doesn't mean it is the right question. God wanted to teach this basic, fundamental lesson to all humanity once and for all—that the questions that start with *why* may never be answered. This is why He allowed the most beautiful Person of all time to ask "Why?" and teach us that the Almighty God does not need to answer.

So long as the *why* is unanswered, we are compelled to trust God in times of agonizing mystery. If and when acceptable answers could be offered by the eternal God to His human creatures in suffering, we would know the meaning of pain and would become more dependent on always demanding answers; we would become even more addicted to reason—and that road leads to the atrophy of faith.

We must come to the mental maturity that confronts agonizing mysteries with the positive attitude: "I don't understand—but I believe in God anyway."

Faith grows through trusting God when we can't see or find answers.

———◇———

Mystery Is the Ultimate Reality

What, after all, is a mystery?

- A mystery is recognizing realities that defy explanation.

- A mystery is asking questions that cannot be answered.

- A mystery is confronting challenges that confound empirical analysis.

- A mystery is the humble confession that we don't have all the answers, and some of our answers may be wrong.

A mystery is a gift of God's grace. It's His strategy to shape us into maximum personhood by molding us into positive-thinking individuals. That means we move into mental maturity when we are shaped into a character who "keeps on keeping on," "moves ahead," "waits patiently," and "trusts anyway." That's the process of growing into mature adulthood! So every mystery is a God-given opportunity to become a bigger, better, and more spiritually mature person.

—◇—

The Questions God Answers

We often ask: "When will help come?" "When will this pain cease?" "When will my faltering faith be restored?" *When?* was the question asked again and again by the Old Testament prophets who wondered if God had forsaken them.

God makes no promise to answer the *when* question, for the same reason God never answers the *why* question—He knows we could not understand and would not accept His answer. We would only argue instead of trusting patiently and quietly.

God has never—anywhere in the Bible—promised to answer these three questions: *why? where?* and *when?* Questions that start with these words are seldom answered.

But God hears and answers questions beginning with *how?* or *what?* These questions sincerely seek wisdom and guidance.

How, O Lord, can I handle this? *How* can I go on positively? *How,* O Lord, can I believe that You do know me and care about me? *How* can I turn my hurts into a halo? And, *How* will You help me to become a better person through my pain?

What? is another question God often answers. Questions that start with *what*—like questions that start with *how*—are humble questions that, instead of provoking argument, sincerely suggest a willingness to invite and follow divine guidance. God promises to give us guidance, often with a holy hint from heaven.

◆

The Mind of God

Benjamin [Hirsch] was a child during the Holocaust. He tells an insightful story about Baal Shem-Tov, the great rabbi who is considered to be the founder of the Hasidic movement. Baal Shem-Tov was standing high on a hill with a couple of his students, looking down at the town where his school was. Suddenly, a group of Cossacks on horseback attacked the town.

As the rabbi saw many of his students along with the men, women, and children of the town being slaughtered, Baal Shem-Tov looked up to heaven and said, "Oh, if only I were God."

One of his students said, with astonishment, "But, Master, if you were God, what would you do differently?"

The reply was, "If I were God, I would do nothing differently. If I were God, I would understand."

We tend to expect to be inspired through reading the Bible, or through creative and inspirational work, but we don't expect to be inspired through pain and hurt. Many of us, like Hirsch, sense a mysterious stirring within us. It is a stirring that tells us that something larger than us is at work, that something is filling our spirits and inspiring us to press on.

We will never be able to understand a gun pointed at an infant's head, or the loss and cruelty experienced during the Holocaust. But, like Hirsch, we may be able to understand—in hindsight or as it happens—that God is present in our blessings and in our trials.

The View from the Valley

The ultimate reality is what lies beyond death. There is a transcending life and a world "out there." We live in a spiritual universe. . . .

One of my dear friends, John Wimber, is in heaven today. John was a great secular musician with the Righteous Brothers and was very, very successful. Then he found faith and began thinking about God and Jesus Christ, and he became a believer. He started reading the Bible and was impressed with how Jesus performed miracles. People who were sick were healed. So John started his own little church to pray for the sick to be healed, and to pray for miracles. That ministry, known as the Vineyard Ministry, is around the world today.

When John became ill with cancer, he used all the medical help available, and his people around the globe prayed for the miracle of healing, which was such a trademark of his ministry. But God didn't answer their prayers with a yes. The cancer returned, and this time it would be terminal. John was able to go back into his pulpit with his cancer still very alive. On his first Sunday back he said, "I have been in the valley, and I can tell you the view from the valley is not too bad." . . .

Some of you don't like this ending. You prayed. You believed. Your heart was torn to pieces. You tried to trust. But it all ended. Death. Divorce. "Life's not fair," you say with a touch of bitterness.

"True," I reply, adding, "life's not fair—but God is good."

Give God more time. Life's too short for all scores to be settled.

—◆—

Lambs Among Wolves

Make no mistake about it—as Christians we are surrounded by enemies! We are Christians in a pagan world! Not long ago I sat in a meeting and listened to a prominent psychologist who declared that Moses was a schizophrenic, that the Bible is a completely discredited book, that God does not exist, and, to cap his demonic lecture, he blasphemed the name of Jesus—and the crowd applauded! This was the first experience in my life when I really felt that I was surrounded by enemies. It is seldom that obvious!

But we must always remember that as Christians we are surrounded by a sinful world bent on destroying God in any form. And if God appears in your life, be sure that the sinful forces of this world will spare no effort to destroy the image of God within you. Usually the enemy is so subtle that we do not sense the danger. . . .

Perhaps our greatest danger is that we are not aware of the peril. There are times in our lives when we do not feel the vile breath of the enemy hot on our back. The world looks so friendly; we feel no need for prayer; the enemy has apparently fled. But watch out! This is only a dangerous peace offensive. This is not the warm wind of spring but a cruelly disarming wind of winter. A tender wind in January may tragically deceive the trees and cause them to send out premature buds with great energy. Suddenly, however, the wind blows cold again, and the shivering trees, unable to cover their tender young buds, freeze in the returning winter storm. . . . The enemy is around us and the enemy is sin! "I send you forth as sheep in the midst of wolves," Jesus said.

—◈—

Be Prepared

We make a grave mistake if we assume that we will never face persecution simply because we live in a free country. There is a strong probability that *all* of us will face some kind of persecution at one time or another in our lives. And it is vitally important to spiritually arm ourselves with inner emergency equipment *before* the crises hit.

Most of us have emergency equipment in our homes and offices—a first-aid kit, a flashlight, perhaps a fire extinguisher, at least a telephone with which to call an emergency unit. We prepare for emergencies before they hit, for we never know when they will come and what they will do to us.

As we need to be prepared with physical equipment, we also need to be prepared spiritually *before* times of persecution arrive. We do that by spending time daily—or, at the very least, weekly—in positive praying, positive Bible study, and worshiping regularly at a positive-thinking church. We saturate our subconscious minds with positive Bible verses, positive hymns, and examples of people who made it through trials successfully, with their faith intact.

—◆—

Persevere in Doing What Is Right

The temptations to "become like" the nonreligious persons around us can be terribly intimidating! . . . To my Christian reader: a warning! Compromise and abandon your principles, and you will literally lose your soul; you'll no longer be the person you were before. You will have lost your identity as a distinctive, independent person. . . . A little bit of you dies every time you surrender a cherished ideal, abandon a noble value, or discard a moral principle.

How do we stand up against social persecution? Once there was a politician who did the best job he could. But, being human, he made mistakes and was criticized, and reporters repeated errors of fact about him in the paper. Well, he became so upset that he drove out into the country to visit his dear friend, a farmer. "What am I going to do?" the politician cried. "I've tried so hard. Nobody has tried harder than I have to do more good for more people—and look how they criticize me!"

But the old farmer could hardly hear the complaint of his persecuted politician friend because his hound dog was barking at the full moon. The farmer rebuked his dog, but the dog kept barking. Finally the farmer said to the politician, "Do you want to know how you should handle your unfair critics? Here's how. Listen to that dog. Now, look at that moon. And remember that people will keep yelling at you—they'll nip at your heels, and they'll criticize you. But here's the lesson: *the dog keeps howling, but the moon keeps shining!*"

Let people persecute you—but don't stop doing all the good you've been doing.

—◇—

Accept God's Help

Persecuted? Facing enormous adversity? Then don't lash out. Don't reject the help God offers. Grasp His helping hand and fall to your knees in prayer. Thank God for the help that He is giving you and will continue to give you. Ask Him to send companions who can help. Ask Him for a supernatural strength to believe and to rejoice anyway!

Possibility Thinking can turn persecution into opportunities for healing . . . for forgiveness . . . for compassion.

———◈———

Turn Trials into Triumphs

Persecution is never eternal. To recover from persecution, be prepared to pass through three phases. The first phase is *collision*. This is the phase that occurs when the consciousness of the awful reality of the situation really hits you. Your peace suddenly clashes with conflict. This is the phase when you realize this horrible thing that is happening is not a dream. It's really happening—to *you!*

The second phase is *withdrawal*. When you talk about fear, guilt, hatred, or anger, all of these emotions are expressions of the tendency to retreat, recoil, withdraw from accepting the horrible reality.

Collision is the first stage. Withdrawal is the second. Phase three is *adjustment*. In this third phase, you finally learn how to accommodate yourself to the loss. The only way you can reach this phase is to realize where you came from, who gave you what you have.

"The Lord gave . . ." Everything you have is from God. Your very life is from God. But not as a gift, mind you. For life is not a gift from God; it is a sacred trust! . . .

It is possible! No matter how great, how deep, how bitter the suffering—when we turn our trials over to Jesus, He can turn them into triumphs! He can do the impossible. He can work miracles. And he can carry us through the phase of collision and withdrawal into the healing phase of acceptance, if we but let Him.

We Follow a Scarred Captain

[Jesus] gave hope to the hopeless, comfort to the comfortless, mercy to those whose hearts and lives were breaking all around them. He gave them the gift of abundant life and the secret of happy living through the Beatitudes:

"Blessed are the poor in spirit, for theirs is the kingdom of heaven."

"Blessed are those who mourn, for they shall be comforted."

"Blessed are the meek, for they shall inherit the earth."

"Blessed are those who hunger and thirst for righteousness, for they shall be satisfied."

"Blessed are the merciful, for they shall obtain mercy."

"Blessed are the pure in heart, for they shall see God."

"Blessed are the peacemakers, for they shall be called children of God."

"Blessed are those who are persecuted for righteousness' sake, for theirs is the kingdom of heaven. Blessed are you when men revile you and persecute you and say all kinds of evil against you falsely on my account. Rejoice and be glad, for your reward is great in heaven."

When Jesus spoke those words, was He thinking about His own persecution that lay ahead? Oh, yes, for surely no one has endured more persecution than Jesus. Surely we follow a scarred captain. He leads us nowhere that He has not walked Himself.

—◆—

What Is This Thing Called Hope?

Hope. It is a marvelous, mysterious mood that comes into your personality. Suddenly your load is lifted, color returns to your skin, and your eyes get their sparkle back. What is it? It is a scientific experience of the presence of God operating in your personality.

Are you an agnostic or an atheist? You say you don't believe in God? Wait a minute. God believes in you. You have had times when you were in despair and you got through it. Somebody or something came and encouraged you. Or you got a bright idea. Or things changed. Or you got lucky. Again and again your good luck was really your good Lord.

You may not believe in Him, but God believes in you, even if you are an atheist. He is not going to cast you out without offering you hope. Hope is a mystery. When it happens in the personality, it can only be scientifically described as the presence of a God of love coming into your mind, your spirit, your body, your personality! This is God. This is hope!

Choose to Be Hopeful

You can choose to be hopeful in your hurt, for never before in history has there been a day like tomorrow. Tomorrow has never before happened.

And tomorrow will be different than today or yesterday. Yes, yesterday is gone. Tomorrow is coming on. And tomorrow is a gift! We pay no fee for each new day. The sunrise is free!

Tomorrow may even be better than you can imagine. Yes, today is pregnant with tomorrow! Tomorrow is inevitable—nothing can delay its arrival. And tomorrow is only a few hours away.

The only thing between today and tomorrow is tonight. And that's when the stars come out!

So never give up on hope! Don't drop the curtain on tomorrow.

Great people are ordinary people who just will not give up hope. And what is hope? It is **H**olding **O**n, **P**raying Expectantly.

———◈———

You Need Hope

You need hope when . . . you get a dream. Whether you are a child, a young person, or an older person, hope lifts that dream until drive and energy come into your personality, and you go for it and take a chance. You need hope when you're dreaming of your future.

You need hope when . . . these dreams run into despairing problems, obstacles, difficulties, and frustrations. You need hope to protect you from the assault of anger, fear, worry, or anxiety. You need hope when you're moving your dreaming into actions.

You need hope when . . . you're healthy. And you need it when you're in ill health.

You need hope when . . . you apply for college and after you're in the university. Then when you choose a career, you will need hope to lift you and lead you onward and upward and forward.

You need hope when . . . you're young and are looking for a girl-friend or boyfriend. And then, when you fall in love, you need it to propose marriage. When you get married, you need hope as much as, if not more than, ever. Hope is what you need when the baby comes and you hold that infant in your arms.

You need hope when . . . you're dying. And you need hope in all of your living.

There will be no love without it. Hope is what will keep your faith alive. That's why hope is right in the middle of the holy trinity of human emotions, "faith, hope, and love."

◆

A Prayer for Hope

I have a strong, serene feeling that
God is planning something good for me today.
I cannot explain it, but I have a deep feeling
that wonderful things are in store for me.
I am expecting God to surprise me with his tender mercy.
He will turn my hurts into halos.
He is guiding my life in such a way that
whatever happens to me will prove to be a beautiful blessing.
Thank you, Lord.
Amen.

———◆———

Choose Hope

Yes, I believe God is still alive. He knows where I am and how I got here. He's way ahead of me, maneuvering in the silence and the shadows. He really cares. I trust Him. The alternative is an unthinkable, unacceptable mental attitude that's certain to lead me down a path of hopeless despair.

Yes! I'm addicted to hope. That's my *decision*. My hopes may not be completely fulfilled, but at least they're keeping me alive and alert and pragmatic. Hope promises to generate and sustain life (and then does). Despair promises to generate and deliver depression and death (and then does). I'd rather choose *hope* (an emotional reaction that promises life but can't guarantee that all of its promises will be fulfilled) than choose *despair* (an emotional reaction that guarantees that its promises of failure and death will surely be kept!).

—◆—

Attitude of Gratitude

The attitude of gratitude gives you surviving power, which means you will not quit.

I was born and raised on an Iowa farm. I vividly remember the dust bowl years. When I was a child, in the thirties, the wind swept in from the Dakotas. It was dry, dusty, violent, and fierce. The wind became our enemy because it would peel off the dry, rich, black soil and swirl it like drifting dunes in the gullies and canyons of our fields. I shall never forget one particularly difficult year. We walked around our farm with white towels over our faces to keep from suffocating in the choking dust.

Then harvest season came. My father would normally harvest a hundred wagonfuls of corn, but that year he harvested not the usual one hundred loads but a meager half wagonload. I can still see the old wagon standing in the yard—only half full. It was a total crop failure, one that has never been equaled.

I shall never forget how, seated at the dinner table with his callused hands holding ours, my father looked up and thanked God. He said, "I thank you, God, that I have *lost nothing*. For I have regained the seed I planted in the springtime." He used half a wagonload for seed; he got half a wagonload back.

His attitude of gratitude was that he had lost nothing while other farmers were complaining that they had lost ninety loads or one hundred loads. *They counted their losses by what they hoped they could have harvested.*

I'll always remember my father saying, "You can never count up the might-have-beens or you will be defeated." Never look at what you have lost; look at what you have left.

—◇—

Out of Tragedy, Gratitude

I recall again how I saw the attitude of gratitude release driving power in my father. It was the time a tornado dropped without warning like a slithering snake out of the black sky and wormed its way toward our farm house. We jumped into our car and escaped with our lives. But the black, serpentine cloud dropped its poisonous head and sucked up all of our nine buildings. It left our farm totally destroyed! The night after the disaster a prayer meeting was held in a little country church, where I heard my father pray, "O God, I thank you that not a life was lost, not a human bone was broken. We have lost nothing that cannot be recaptured and regained. And through the storm we have kept everything that would have been irreplaceable—especially our faith."

That attitude of gratitude gave my father driving power. It gave him enthusiasm. We went to town and bought the remnants of an old four-story house that was, for many months, in the process of being dismantled—sold section by section the way a four-layer chocolate cake is sold by the slice. One last section still stood waiting to be bought for fifty dollars by someone who would be willing to remove it. So we bought it and began, carefully and tediously, to dismantle it nail by nail, board by board. We hauled each shingle and plank to the place where our farm had stood and began to rebuild a new home over the empty hole in the ground that was the basement of our previous house. When we focused on what we could do, rather than on what we had lost, we became grateful once more. And that released the energy to climb up and onward!

—◇—

Thanks for Gifts Spiritual

Be thankful for prayers answered, known and unknown. Discouraged? Stop! Think about all the prayers God has answered for you in the past. Some of these prayers that have been answered are prayers that you didn't pray. Others were praying for you: friends, parents, grandparents. Maybe you sat on your grandpa or your grandma's knee and they were praying for you. Do you realize that prayers are seeds? And they can last a long, long time. One day, given the right environment, they sprout.

I remember my first trip to Cairo, Egypt. In the museum you can see kernels of wheat that were taken from King Tut's tomb. That tomb pre-dates Jesus Christ by centuries. Some of these kernels of wheat were taken out of the museum and in fact they sprouted! They are not dead! Just because they didn't sprout earlier doesn't mean they are dead. God's delays are not God's denials.

Be thankful for prayers answered: known and unknown. Be thankful for seeds that will sprout with enough patience and tender loving care.

Be thankful for sins forgiven, both public and private. We all have committed sins that people know about and sins that nobody knows about and may never discover, but are known only to you, your conscience, and your God. So when a disappointment hits, no matter what it is, a broken relationship, a financial disaster, you can be happy if you can go to bed at night, put your head on the pillow, and know God loves you and forgives you. God thinks you are fantastic! He is your best friend.

—◇—

Thanks for Life Restored

Be thankful for healings, seen and unseen. You can see scars. You can recall the surgery. There are known and obvious symbols of healing. But pause and think a minute of all the hidden hurts, the unrevealed wounds, the quiet, little secret torturing memories that you carried with you—and then there was that moment when you dropped them and God touched you and healed you of your hurt. You were grateful then. And you can begin to be thankful now because God won't let you down. He healed you yesterday; He will also do it today.

Be thankful for the storms of your life that have blown out, blown over, or passed you by and never touched you. Give thanks to God for all the narrow escapes you'll never know about. You and I will never know how often our lives have been spared, how close we came to being at the intersection when the accident happened and we could have been involved. You will never know in your life what infectious germs touched your body but never took root so you never became ill! Yes, thank God for storms which blew out, blew over, passed you by, never touched you. God shows His goodness to you in many ways.

———◆———

Thanks for Life's Gifts

Be thankful for friends, old and new. When disappointments hit, stop and recall old friends. If you're down and discouraged, take time and write on a piece of paper the friends that have meant the most to you in your life. Go back to your childhood: Who was the little girl or the little boy you walked to school with? Who was your favorite teacher? Who was the favorite friend on your block? Who was the schoolmate? Think of all these friends, the old ones, the present ones, and the new ones, and then stop and think: "Some of the best friends in your life you haven't even met yet!" Surely the love of friends is like the hand of God reaching out to comfort you. . . .

Be thankful for gifts, given and received. Pause and think about the gifts you've received, but most of all, thank God for the joy of giving. Early in our ministry, my wife would urge me at times of discouragement to call on members of the church who were shut in. I would visit them and give them an uplifting, encouraging thought. In the process, I discovered a really great truth: it is impossible to give of yourself without receiving something immediately. "Do not fret because of evil doers. Trust in the LORD, and do good" (Ps. 37:1, 3).

—◆—

Thanks for Possibilities

Be thankful for impossibilities that became possibilities. It is easy to forget past blessings. We can get so blinded by something that isn't happening today that we focus on the unanswered prayers instead of the answered prayers. We look at what is denied us instead of what we have left. We get hung up on our failures instead of on our triumphs, our successes, and our achievements. God says to us, "Be thankful always for all good things."

Think of the impossibilities that became possibilities. When I become discouraged, I come and stand in [the Crystal] Cathedral and remember when this fantastic building was just one great big, wild, impossible idea! Engineers told me, "You can't build a building out of glass that big in an earthquake zone."

But we did it and it has survived some pretty good shakes. Thank God for impossibilities that became possibilities. . . .

Be thankful for possibilities that God put within you. There are possibilities within each of us that have been discovered and developed. There are others that remain undiscovered, undeveloped, and give me the frontier edge of potential progress in the weeks and months to come. So, be thankful for possibilities that are blossoming. Be thankful that the world hasn't seen the best of you yet. If you're not happy with what you see, stick around. God is still at work.

—◆—

Unblock the Power of Gratitude

Begin by saying thank you to the persons who live with you and work with you. Each day mention a specific quality of work or attitude they display that is helpful to you. Let others know how much you appreciate them. Carry a diary of gratitude with you everywhere you go and record all the nice experiences that happen, the nice people you meet. It is amazing to contemplate the powers you will unlock and release within yourself with this discipline. The attitude of gratitude begins each day with the feeling, "Thank God for letting me live today" and each new day begins anew with a peak to peek experience.

—◇—

The Power of *Thanks!*

Learn the power of the word *Thanks!*

Rudyard Kipling was one of those authors who was very successful in his lifetime. A British newspaper criticized him and ridiculed him and called him a mercenary. They said, "He is now writing just for the money. One word of Rudyard Kipling today is worth a hundred dollars."

Shortly after the release of the unkind article, a reporter approached Kipling at a gathering and said, "So, you're worth a hundred dollars a word. Here's a hundred dollars. Give me a word." Then he handed him a paper and pencil.

Kipling took the hundred dollars, put it in his pocket, and on the paper he wrote one word: *Thanks!*

Yes, if a disappointment causes you to slip, stumble, and slide into discouragement, then lift your mood back up by giving thanks to God always for all things.

—◇—

Choose the Action,
Choose the Consequences

Listen to the sober warning from the lips of Christ: "He that hears these words of mine and does them not, I will liken him unto a foolish man who built his house on sand, and the rains descended and the floods came and the winds blew and beat upon that house and it fell, and great was the fall of it!"

So sounds the ominous statement of the Savior Himself. Of course, these are not pleasant words. But for the sake of our immortal soul we had better take God's warnings seriously—or suffer the consequences. The height of self-deceit is when a person tells himself that he can sin and that God will automatically forgive and forget—that somehow, "nature" will overlook the whole affair. The terrible truth is that judgment is built into the universe.

—◆—

Sacrificial Love

Again and again I am asked why Christianity uses the cross as its symbol. Is this not a morbid symbol? On the contrary! The cross is an inspiring reminder that God will stop at nothing to save His children.

Why did God have to resort to a cross to redeem us? The answer is obvious if we think about it seriously. Sweet words alone do not redeem people. After Christ delivered the beautiful sermon on the mount people crucified Him! Sweet words may impress people—but only sacrificial love wins disciples! "Love so amazing, so divine, demands my life, my soul, my all." "I, if I be lifted up, will draw all men unto myself" was the prophecy of Jesus Christ. He uttered the most beautiful words ever spoken by a human being; He performed miracles of compassionate healing that have never been equalled; He lived a humble life of devoted service to people of all races and classes, but this was not enough! In the final analysis it would only be through His own self-sacrifice that we would be drawn in complete commitment to His cause. . . .

God cannot promiscuously forgive and irresponsibly overlook evil. Sin must be punished. God is a moral Being. And the cross was God's way of atoning for our sins and redeeming our souls.

—◆—

Without Our Props

An allegory tells about a soul that came to heaven. Just outside of heaven was a huge arena called "The Court of Status Symbols." Before he could get into heaven he had to go through this area, past the keeper of the door of the court. Inside he saw sleek automobiles, membership cards to exclusive clubs, white poodles, silver-tipped canes, etc. As he went farther back into the room he saw the crowns of kings and beautiful jewelry from princesses. Then the guide said, "Yes, these were all things that the world used to impress people, symbols of significance. But they don't impress Him! So we have everybody drop them right here before they come to stand before Him!"

For some people, I submit, to have to stand before God without all of the props that we have been using to impress people might be a nightmare. Or suppose, as a certain theologian suggested, that death is like a dream. Imagine that death will be like falling asleep. Suddenly you awake to an unending dream! We know, of course, that dreams for the most part are exaggerated projections of our past experiences. For one who has lived in the love of God and has thrilled to beautiful music and has felt the wonderful warmth of faith, life after death will be one long, beautiful, unending, and inspiring dream. But for one to whom existence has been nothing more than self-indulgence, feeding the desires of his physical organism which can no longer be fed in eternity, would not the dream be one unending nightmare? So Christ makes the point clear. There is hell; there is heaven.

There Is Life Beyond Hope

There is life beyond hope. Justice demands it. We can't accept an evil man like Hitler using suicide and getting off so easily with death. And we can't believe that God who is just and merciful can allow sin and evil to get by without facing ultimate justice.

God will not allow death to be a loophole! He doesn't close the books on a life that dies. He opens the book of justice and mercy. He reigns eternally and will appropriately reward the faithful and apply justice where it is appropriate.

Give God more time, and eternity will balance everything beautifully.

Prepare to embrace eternity!

I believe that human souls live eternally. I embrace that belief even though I know very little about heaven and hell. But evidence both inside and outside Scripture hints of heaven. . . .

Yes, there is life beyond hope. Yes, there is a God. He will have the last word—and it will be beautiful. Yes, there was a Man of God named Jesus Christ who lived. That's a fact. He died. That's a fact. He was resurrected from the dead. That's a mystery. He is my Lord and Savior. That's my faith. He has promised to all humans: "The one who comes to Me I will by no means cast out" (John 6:37). Holding to that promise, I face death and eternity knowing that I'm going where Jesus already is!

That's eternal life. That's salvation.

---◇---

Your Choice

Your eternity is determined by you in your lifetime. How? By the life you live? To some extent, I suppose, but that is not really all. None of us can really atone for the sins we have committed. Then how can we be redeemed or saved? I know of only one Person in all of human history who ever said, "I am the good shepherd. By me, if any one enter in, he shall be saved." His name is Jesus Christ. . . .

Understand this. God has never sent a single soul to hell. He never has and He never will! Men send themselves there by proudly refusing to accept His gift of love. Christ will save anybody who comes. "You who come to Me," He said, "I shall under no circumstances cast out."

Someday I shall have to cross the dividing line and move to the other side, and so will you. Personally, I anticipate it as the most exciting trip I have ever taken and I anticipate it with more excitement than I did my first around-the-world trip two years ago. "I have no fear, for thou art with me."

"You who come to Me I will in no wise cast out." And what does it mean to come? It doesn't mean just to sit and politely ignore Him. It means to rise up and accept Him. "Someday," John McNeill said, "I will draw my feet into the bed for the last time and turn my face to the wall and I will have to look at the gulf, but my Shepherd and I will look at it together. 'I will not fear for I will hold on to that promise of Jesus Christ and dare to swing out over the wide gulf on that slender rope, knowing that it will not drop me, for it is rooted in God's imperishable love." Take hold of that rope now!

—◇—

Consider the Lilies

Once Christ came to visit the home of Mary and Martha. Martha was so busy in the kitchen with the dishes and the food and the house and the clothes that she thought she had no time to come out to talk to Jesus. She was so concerned about things that she had no time for people, so concerned about her house that she had no time for God. So Jesus said, "Oh, Martha, you are so concerned about so many things, so many things. And only one thing is really needed."

And that is God!

Christ makes this point very clear in the Sermon on the Mount: "Blessed are they that hunger and thirst after righteousness, for they shall be satisfied" (Matt. 5:6).

There you have it—the formula for fulfillment, the key to contentment, the secret of satisfaction.

Do you understand? I hope so. Listen to Jesus: Be not so concerned about things. Do not be so concerned about your house and your clothes. Consider the lilies of the field, how they grow. They toil not, neither do they spin, and yet I say unto you that even Solomon in all his glory was not arrayed like one of these. Seek first the kingdom of God and his righteousness, and all these things will come (Matt. 6:27–33).

The feeling of fulfillment is in finding faith. Most of you understand and know that. You have felt the throb of God in your heart. You have prayed to Him and felt His presence. And these great spiritual experiences are real. No wonder they satisfy.

—◇—

Thou Shalt Not Covet

Do you sometimes sense that you are missing out on something but you don't quite know on what? The person who has inordinate desires and who covets his neighbor's position or property is a person who deep within himself is frustrated.

Now God wants us to live the good life. And if we positively apply these Ten Commandments to daily living, we will enjoy the good life. And if you want to know what is meant by the good life, direct your attention to Jesus Christ. This was the good life incarnate.

What was life like for Him? Take a look at His last days on earth and you will see the secret of His satisfying life. Shortly before He died He said to His apostles, "I would that my joy might be in you and that your joy might be complete" (John 15:11). The good life, then, is a life that has an inner joy.

Then hear this: "Peace I leave with you, my peace I give unto you: not as the world giveth, give I unto you. Let not your heart be troubled, neither let it be afraid" (John 14:27). The good life is a life that has a deep undercurrent of profound peace.

The last words to fall from Christ's lips, as He hung and died under the Jerusalem sky, were short and simple, but triumphant: "It is finished" (John 19:30). He had carried out His divine mission. The good life is the awareness of fulfillment. For "every person's life is a plan of God." God has a plan for you. And the good life is the deep feeling that we are fulfilling God's plan and purpose in our life.

This I submit is the good life: inner joy, deep peace, and a sense of accomplishment.

—◇—

The Tyranny of Things

Materialism does not satisfy because it is tyrannical, and *the human being was born to be free!* We all know about the tyranny of things. We find that we don't own a house—the house owns us. We are married to a mortgage. We become slaves to gadgets and garments. After we have all our "things" purchased, delivered, and installed, and have enjoyed a fleeting sense of pleasure, we find that they are still dominating, dictating, and demanding. "Press me, polish me, patch me, paint me, prune me, plaster me, repair me," they shout. So we spend the best years of our lives and the bulk of our money working for "things," until, discouraged and depressed, we discover that we have no time left to pursue life's really enjoyable avocations: visiting friends, having fun, and, yes, even going to church regularly. Thus mastered by materialism, tyrannized by things, we have no time left to do the deeds, or see the places, or visit the people, that would really give us great inner joy.

—◇—

A Boring Life

To understand the futility of the materialistic life further, we must come to see that materialism begets monotony; and boredom is one of the major obstacles to the good life. Life quickly becomes monotonous. Things rapidly bore us. That is why styles have to change periodically. There has to be the long look, the short look, the baggy look, the sacky look, or the bloated look, but there has to be a *new* look, always. So we have to reupholster, replace, redecorate, or at least rearrange the furniture. Things bore us.

We get a certain amount of excitement in shopping for it, looking for it, waiting for it to be delivered, putting it in just the right place, maybe admiring it for a day or two or three, and then suddenly, days, weeks, months pass and we haven't even been conscious of this "thing" for which we work, slave, and spend our lives. To break our boredom, then, we must get on to a new "kick"—a new-car kick, or a new-carpet kick, a new-job kick—anything! So briefly we break the boredom. Momentarily we have mastered monotony! We have a new interest, a new cause, a new project. . . .

Yes, things bore us because things are dead. They do not talk, or laugh, or love. Man was born for fellowship. We are not happy unless we have friends. Even an argument is better than loneliness.

---◇---

The Object of Our Affection

No one is happy with things because they don't satisfy his or her natural hunger for companionship.

Now there are exceptions, of course. Some "things" really seem to satisfy us. But these are the "objects of affection." It may be a work of art that satisfies us because it speaks of someone's creative talent. It may be a sentimental something which satisfies because it reawakens happy memories and for a moment is a substitute for the real person. Think of some of the things that satisfy: little children's shoes, grandfather's Bible, mother's favorite piece of jewelry, a treasured gift from your true love. But we must understand that the only reason these things seem to satisfy is because we identify them with some person we love, or some experience that was beautiful.

Now we are beginning to see what really satisfies in life. *Love* is the fulfillment of life. For people are born to love. See how brilliant is the insight of Christ into the human heart when He says, "Thou shalt love the Lord thy God with all thy heart and with all thy soul and with all thy mind. This is the first and great commandment. And the second is like unto it—thou shalt love thy neighbor as thyself."

This is why no person will really feel whole and complete until he has met God, for "God is love" (1 John 4:8).

The Riches of Poverty

On a camping trip some years ago, I faced what appeared to be a minor crisis in our family. We were miles from home when it was discovered that my small boy had forgotten to bring his toys. My limited budget left no money to buy my son the sailboat he wanted. We decided to build one. . . . The building of this toy became an exciting family project! It was an unforgettable thrill as the children watched this toy take shape. "Do you think it will really sail, Daddy?" Bobby asked doubtfully. "Of course, Bobby," Sheila rebuked him. Then, with the unshakable confidence of a six-year-old child, she added, "Everything Daddy makes always works." Bobby's eyes sparkled with newly revived faith in the whole project. "Hurry up, Daddy, let's try it," he urged. We jammed the mast in the hull, pinned the sail in place with a safety pin, and headed off for the lake.

There was an appropriate christening ceremony on the shore. We named her "Queen of the Lake." After spending some hectic minutes convincing my youngest that he could not ride on board, we launched her! The sail trembled as fearfully as a child about to take his first step; then, as if gaining sudden confidence, the sail billowed forth, pulling with increasing speed the new Queen across the water on her maiden voyage. "She sails! She sails! She sails!" the children cheered. In that moment I felt rather proud of myself. A lack of money to buy a sailboat opened the way to a great self-exhilarating experience. My somewhat impoverished state gave me a sense of self-esteem which the financial ability to purchase a sleek, perfectly produced boat in a toy store never could have done.

DECEMBER 12

Casting All Your Care Upon Him

The survivors of the tornado in Illinois brought back my memory of a family crisis. . . . when our farm was blown away in a tornado. We scratched through the rubble, hoping to recover some items of value. We found very little. We found a twisted silver spoon, a Bible that belonged to my grandfather. . . . Just as we were beginning to get discouraged, my mother found part of a plastic picture that had hung on our kitchen wall. It had once had the Bible verse on it, "Keep looking to Jesus." The picture was broken in half. We found only the top half. It said simply, "Keep looking."

We thought that was very funny. We did keep looking. We found the back of the piano and many of the strings were still tight. Then we found one item that was unbroken. It was also a plaster of Paris plaque that we had purchased in a religious bookstore and had hung on the wall. It was also a Bible verse: "Casting all your care upon Him, for He cares for you" (1 Pet. 5:7).

Can you imagine the impression that made on a young teenager? My suitcase was still unpacked, having just come home from college for a vacation. My school papers were gone. My beloved riding horse was dead. In the midst of that disaster, we find an unbroken plaster of Paris motto: "Casting all your care upon Him, for He cares for you." The message was burned into me.

I know from firsthand experience that life can be difficult. But I also know that God is good! If you believe that God will guide you and you follow Him in faith, then you will get a new dream, a new idea, a new goal. When that happens, the disappointment has turned into *Hisappointment!* You're on your way to discovering that life's not fair—*but God is good!*

◆

Your Promises, Your Peace

You never promised, Lord, that I would be forever sheltered from stormy times in my life. You have promised that the sun will outlast the storms. You issue the grand command from outer space, and the renegade storm clouds break up, scatter, and flee like hoodlums hurriedly racing from the streets back to their hidden lairs in some forbidden alley.

The bright stars come out to laugh again like children returning once more to safe streets for happy play. The sky clears. The huge yellow moon sails once more, calm and serene, through the silent sky.

Even as you restore peace after the storm, so you will restore a renewed calm to my troubled mind through your peace-instilling presence that is surrounding me now. Your quiet, calming spirit is flowing within me. Thank you, Lord.

Thank you, God, for dangers that teach me to be brave; for suffering from which I learn patience; for pain, which teaches me tenderness; for false friends, whose lack of trust causes me to prize my true friends; for illness, which teaches me to treasure my health, a gift I too often take for granted.

Thank you for leading me through trying times, without which I would be like a plant in an overprotected hothouse, too tender to ever live in the open wind.

Help me to remember in my trying times that there is no progress without pain, no conversion without crisis, no birth without painful travail, no Easter without Good Friday.

Trying times are times to try more faith. I'm trying. I'm believing. You are helping me. Thank you, Lord. Amen

—◆—

Those Who Wait upon the Lord

The storm has passed. The birds are singing. The night is over. Tough times never last. Tough people do! That's really true if we live moment by moment, day by day, in complete surrender to God in prayer. Through prayer, God gives the power to hold on to tough times until the breakthrough comes.

But those who wait on the LORD
Shall renew their strength;
They shall mount up with wings like eagles,
They shall run and not be weary,
They shall walk and not faint. (Isa. 40:31)

I have found immense strength through this promise of God. As I wait upon Him in prayer I find the strength to go on. The terrible danger in tough times is that we lose our emotional power to remain enthusiastic and creative. But the solution God offers is prayer, the power that pulls everything together successfully.

Sacred Resources

When times are the toughest and it seems as if you are as low as you can go and when Possibility Thinking hasn't had the results you expected, you are in danger of burnout. It's precisely at these times you need God because when you remain in touch with God, you are immune to burnout. You say, "But don't you get terribly down at times?" Yes, but remember I said you can be immune to *burnouts*, not *brownouts*. A brownout is a temporary power failure. It is not a permanent resignation, divorce, or bill of sale. You may feel down in a brownout, but you don't abandon the ship as you would in a burnout. It's important to know the difference. In a brownout the power will come back on. A burnout? That's a toughie. To keep a brownout from becoming a burnout you must remain in touch with God—and that's what prayer is. But remember, keeping in touch with God won't eliminate your problems . . . it will only help you manage them. The late comedian Grady Nutt said it: "God should be a resource in the struggle, not a way around it."

Nourishment from Above

Wait on the Lord, and *He will renew Your strength!*

Prayer is the umbilical cord that allows you—with your embryonic ideas—to draw nourishment from a source that you, like an unborn infant, can neither see nor fully know or comprehend—God our heavenly Father! Prayer is the power that pulls everything together successfully.

With this prayerful attitude, tackle your problem today. Turn it over to God. Take out a sheet of paper. Pick up a pencil. And get ready for the ideas that He will drop into your mind.

Father, I have a strong sensation
that you brought me to this moment of prayer
because you plan to share with me insights to solve my problems.
So I will go out and face the sunlight of a new day
and a new week crammed with undiscovered possibilities.
I am encouraged! I am enthused!
I am more hopeful than I have been in a long time!
Amen.

◆

Wait on the Lord

True prayer will bring renewal.

Pray—and wait! *Wait*—this is the painful but power-packed word. Somewhere John Henry Jowett has reminded us that "God gives us the grace to move ahead, to back up, to stand up, and also to sit still and wait." "Wait on the Lord . . . and He shall strengthen thine heart: wait, I say, on the Lord." Have you prayed and there is no change? Then turn your face to the east, your thoughts to springtime, and your heart to God, and wait.

"How long must I wait?" you ask. Greater saints than you have asked that question. The patience of God is terrifying. The slowness of His providence is torturing. For we are still very childish in our concept of time. A year seems like an age to a young man. We must mature like old men—when a year does not seem long anymore.

How long? The Psalmist asked: "Return, O Lord, how long?" Isaiah as well as that discouraged prophet Jeremiah raised the question. And when Jeremiah realized that the battle would be longer than expected he wisely advised, "This captivity is long, build your houses!" For some of us our battle is going to be long. Begin digging and laying spiritual foundations, and build a house of faith and prayer or you will never be able to stick it out! *God has never promised that He would hurry up!*

—◇—

A New Awareness

Does God seem far from you today? Wait and pray. God will visit you again! "His going forth shall be as sure as the morning."

Why am I so sure? Because God has promised this. "Say to them that are of a fearful heart, Be strong, fear not: behold, your God will come with vengeance, even God with a recompense; he will come and save you.... In the wilderness shall waters break out, and streams in the desert.... And the ransomed of the Lord shall return ... with songs and everlastingly joy upon their heads: they shall obtain joy and gladness, sorrow and sighing shall flee away" (Isa. 35:4–10).

"I waited patiently for the Lord. He inclined unto me and heard my cry. He lifted me up out of the pit and put my feet upon a rock. He established my goings and put a new song in my heart, even praise unto my God" is the testimony of another saint.

Deep within myself I have a powerful awareness that I have
made the right decision and am moving in the right direction.
I will let nothing and no one deter, detour,
distract, depress, or defeat me.
"No man having put his hand to the plow
and looking back is fit for the kingdom of God."
God's spirit is rising within me now, making me very
determined to faithfully keep the beautiful promises I've made.
I will be faithful. I am reliable.
Thank you, God.
Amen.

◆

Your Hallelujah Returns

Do you feel your spiritual life has lost its luster? Has your religion lost its reality? Are prayer, God, Christ, unreal?

Today, if there are birds winging and you do not see them, children singing and you do not hear them, flowers blooming and you do not enjoy them, God moving and you do not feel Him—keep waiting, keep praying! God will not mock your waiting. God will not laugh at your praying. God will not be deaf to your pleading. Suddenly you hear footsteps in the hall and your prison door swings open, and you are free again!

"Sometimes a light surprises a Christian while he sings! It is the Lord who comes with healing on His wings." Restored! And there is a new bloom on the rose, a sharp edge on the knife; trumpet tones are clear again; the enemy raises a white flag; crocuses bloom through the snow; streams break out in the desert; the moon sails calm again as God returns to the waiting heart!

You rejoice! Your hallelujah has returned to your heart! "They that wait upon the Lord shall renew their strength, they shall mount up with wings like eagles, . . . they shall run and not faint!" Amen, Amen, and Hallelujah!

—◈—

I Am Waiting

Thank you, Lord, for your messages
that come from the deepest, unexplored,
unfathomable seas of silence.
Through beautiful, positive thoughts
you come into my mind.
Oh, Lord, it is going to be a great day!
I am waiting. I am ready.
I am listening. I will move.
Amen.

Listen to Him

Do you want a satisfying life, a life without that hollow feeling, that empty feeling, that purposeless kind of an existence that you sometimes sense? Then the answer is: God, and nothing else— nothing else! And you will find God when you come to Jesus Christ. So often people have said to me, "Well, if there is a God, why haven't we seen Him? If there is a God, why hasn't He given us an opportunity to look at Him?" I have pointed out that He has done this. . . . Once He has drawn the curtain and lifted the veil and given us a glimpse of what He is really like by coming down to our level.

King James of Scotland used to dress in the clothes of a peasant from time to time and then walk through the villages and the countryside. Nobody knew that this was the king. He did this in order that he might find out how the people were thinking, what their agonies were, what their heartaches and their problems amounted to. He was a king getting down to the people's level.

I believe that Jesus Christ was God visiting the world. . . .

Let us listen to His own testimony. He says, "I am the light of the world." What a statement! What a claim! If He is not telling the truth, then He is making a most boastful claim, is He not?

Listen to Him when He says, "I am the vine, you are the branches. Except you abide in me, you can do nothing." Listen to Him when He says, "The son of man has power to forgive sins." What authority! What a divine declaration of His preeminent position!

God's Visit

The greatest news in the world is that God has visited this earth. He has walked this planet. He has made His great pronouncements. He has uttered His voice. He has spoken His mind. He has declared His will. He has revealed His heart.

It is Jesus who reveals to the human race that God is "the eye that never closes, the ear that is never shut, the mind that never stops thinking, the heart that never grows cold."

God would be only a vague idea, an irresponsible product of someone's imagination, an unreliable exercise of human philosophizing, if it were not for Jesus Christ. Interpret Jesus as you wish, but one fact emerges clearly—God becomes real to those who draw close to Christ. So listen to Him when He says: "Come unto me, all you who labor and are heavy-laden. Come unto me, and I will give you rest." Come unto me, you with the empty, hollow lives. And when you come, don't intellectualize, analyze, or diagnose Him. Simply bow; simply believe; simply bend your knee. Here's to a good life for you!

———◆———

"Lo, I am with you always . . ."

Christ portrays a God who guides us through life, provides us with what we need, and *abides with us forever*. There is no promise that God will never allow His children to experience pain, or suffering, or even fall victim to natural catastrophes. But there is the promise that He will be with us always and everywhere. The Psalmist knew this. And he said, "Yea, though I walk through the valley of the shadow of death, I will fear no evil: *for thou art with me.*"

Hear the Word of the Lord: "Fear not; for I have redeemed you, I have called you by your name and you are mine! When you pass through the waters . . . they shall not overflow you . . . fear not, for I am with you" (Isa. 43:1, 2, 5).

Once [David] Livingstone was asked how he was able to face the steaming jungles, months of loneliness, dangers of beast, serpent, insect, disease, and savages. The great missionary testified to the University of Glasgow where he was receiving an honorary degree of Doctor of Laws, "Would you like me to tell you what supported me through all the years of exile among people whose language I could not understand, and whose attitude toward me was always uncertain and often hostile? It was this—" He paused reverently. His left arm, crushed by a lion's jaws, hung limp and helpless at his side. Then he continued—"It was this, 'Lo, I am with you always, even unto the end of the world.' On these words I staked everything, and they never failed!"

Come close, friend. Draw near, neighbor. Follow me, wayfarer. Take a serious, sincere, and searching look at Christ, and you will have an authentic image of the eternal God. And while you look, bend your knee and kneel.

—◇—

Lord, Show Us the Father

So you rightly and wisely ask, How can I know what God is like? What image can I intelligently believe to be an authentic impression, a responsible representation, a reliable image? . . . Behold the Babe of Bethlehem.

God came down and walked around on this earth in a human body. And He was called Jesus! This Christ is not an ordinary itinerant preacher. This is God putting Himself in our shoes. It was the only way God could "get through" to the human race.

Father Damian, you remember, was a great missionary to the lepers. From the first he called them his brothers and sisters. But he did not establish a real rapport with them until years later, when he addressed them with the words, "We lepers"! Christ was God, getting down to our level. The Babe in the manger is God wrapped in a blanket—royalty in rags. The stranger of Galilee performing those unexplainable miracles (which even His enemies never doubted or disqualified)—this tall man with the compassionate heart—is God with a robe on, God with sandals on His feet, God eating bread and drinking water and becoming tired. This is God, putting Himself into our shoes in order to portray clearly to the human family what He, the Eternal, is really like!

Once, Phillip asked Jesus, "Lord, show us the Father," and Jesus replied, "Have I been so long a time with you, and yet have you not known me, Phillip? [H]e that has seen me has seen the Father" (John 14:9).

Yes, draw close to Christ and you will see the perfect portrait, the only divinely approved image of the Almighty God.

A Christmas Prayer

You lead me, Jesus Christ, to thoughts of God.
I see you in a manger carved from a tree.
I see you as a young man with hands that
   reach to touch hearts that hurt.
Your caring reaches out like the strong and
   kind branches of a gentle tree reach out
   to invite road-weary and travel-worn wayfarers
   to quiet rest.
I see you again hanging on a tree with outstretched
   arms taking in the whole world.
From your cross, you show me that God will stop at
   nothing to save my soul.
So, I celebrate God's love today as I celebrate
   your birth around a twinkling Christmas tree.
I pray my life, like yours, O Lord, may be tall
   and upright as a pine tree pointing, reaching,
   sharing, sparkling, life-giving; solid, sturdy,
   strong-rooted in God's love, a beautiful soul,
   evergreen forever.
Amen.

DECEMBER 26

Nothing Is Impossible

Manage your time, and you'll manage to succeed in accomplishing what appear to be impossible goals.

Nothing is impossible! Some things just take a long—or longer!—time.

Nothing is impossible! I just have to learn when and what to delegate to whom.

Nothing is impossible! I just have to make better use of my hours and years.

What goals could you achieve if you blocked out ten years? Fifteen years? Twenty years? Thirty years? Forty years? Move your thinking from a clock to a calendar. Then *nothing* is impossible!

Time is the one thing that can't be replaced.

Value Time

We tend to waste what we value too lightly. Though it has been said often, every successful person knows it is true that time is money. It can be invested or spent unwisely. Properly invested it is available to create ideas, organize plans, invent new products, study problems, or acquire knowledge, information, or experience, all leading to higher levels of achievement.

Perhaps we would treasure time more highly if we had to pay a tax on wasted time. Perhaps we would make better use of our time if we had to pay for the privilege of living. But time seems to come to us without charge—absolutely free! . . .

We also tend to undervalue and consequently waste a commodity whenever there seems to be an overabundance. Too many people seem to assume that they will live almost forever. There will be "plenty of time" to achieve something worthwhile before they finally pass off this earth. Thus the years pass and with them ripe opportunities.

Early in life my mother drummed this sentence into my mind: "Lost time is never found again." . . .

So value time the way you value gold and life itself.

—◈—

The Habit of Time Accounting

Nothing is more important, or more valuable to you, than your time. Yet have you ever made a careful accounting of how you spend it? . . .

Analyze your time expenditures. Get a notebook and keep an accurate record for a month. How much time do you spend dressing? Eating? Drinking? Praying? Reading? Body grooming? Cleaning? Repairing? Shopping? Visiting? Make a detailed study. You will be amazed at some of your hard factual findings. You will begin to understand the problem of time in modern life. You will discover that overly much time is spent painting, patching, pruning, pressing, packing, unpacking, and repairing.

When you finish your study, you may be forced to make some drastic decisions about your life. You surely will be better prepared to budget your time wisely and fruitfully.

It has been observed that time is a bigger problem today than a century ago. Isn't that peculiar—with all of our rapid means of communication and timesaving devices? After you account for your time you may find the reasons for this phenomenon. My father and mother lived in the age between the horse and buggy and automobile. Because they lived in the country and started life with the horse and buggy, they went to town only once a week. They made all of their purchases on that one trip. The round trip to town took one hour. They spent sixty minutes a week traveling to the store. How much time do you spend in one week traveling from your house to the car to the store, and back again?

—◆—

Is It Time to Reorganize?

Whether you've failed or succeeded, chances are there are parts of your life that need reorganization. The only person who doesn't have to reorganize constantly is the person for whom life and business have become static. Anybody whose life is static is dead.

I've been reorganizing the past month. I took a few days off with my wife and we prayed. I asked these questions, to myself, to God, to my wife:

- Who am I?

- Where have I come from?

- How did I get here?

- Where do I want to go?

- How can I get there?

I knew who I was last month, and last year, but I'm constantly changing. I need to frequently reevaluate who I am and where I am going. And right now I'm reorganizing my life around the answers to those questions. . . .

Reorganize. Times change. You may have to change your whole corporate structure. You may have to abolish some departments. Sometimes you have to go back to get on the right track. Maybe you need to advance. Perhaps you need to retreat or regroup. Maybe you need to scale your operation up or down, maybe even close down. Whatever your situation is, chances are that you need to reorganize.

———◇———

The Psalmist's Faith
(The 23rd Psalm)

What does the Psalmist mean by saying that goodness and mercy will follow him all the days of his life? He is saying that he has no anxiety or fear of the future. He is convinced that in the providence of God the future will be friendly.

Fear poverty? No—"The Lord is my shepherd. I shall not want." Fear loneliness? No—"For thou art with me." Fear a nervous breakdown? No—"He will make me to lie down in green pastures beside still waters." Fear falling into terrible sin? No—"Thy rod and thy staff they comfort me." Fear making bad judgments? No—"He leadeth me." Fear life, death, and eternity? No—"I shall dwell in the house of the Lord for ever."

"Surely goodness and mercy shall follow me all the days of my life." Sweet words! Like the note of a nightingale, or gentle music that falls from a harp! Strong words! Like a chorus of men's voices singing on Easter morning. Triumphant words! Like a great pipe organ swelling to full power in the mighty closing moments of a thrilling magnificat!

The Psalmist claims that he is not afraid of the future because he believes that God is good. For many of us this is easy to believe. We count our blessings—blessings of country, family, friends, eyes, hands, and ears. The goodness of God is very conspicuous to His unspoiled children.

⬥

To Feel the Presence of God

As a great wave rises from the deep to wash away the scratches on the sand, come, O God, to dissolve forever in your sea of peace my cares, my fears, my worries, and my anxieties.

As the blessed blackness of a quiet night comes to blanket from my sight the cluttered collection of billboards, buildings, and power poles until my eyes see only bright stars, so come, O God, and blot out this day's dreary and weary accumulations of daily irritations, hurts, dents, and disappointments until I see only your goodness shining in the shadows.

As an explosion of happy sunshine brings a joyful glow to dark corners, so come, O God, and explode your bright joy into the gloomy corners of my mind.

As a great victorious general awakens his battalions with a trumpet blast, and rallies his retreating army with renewing power, so come, O Lord, and awaken me to "rise up, be done with lesser things, to give heart, soul, mind, and strength to serve the King of Kings."

As the spring rain gently, patiently, irresistibly falls to soften the hard crust of frozen ground until it can receive fruit-producing seed, so, O God, may showers of your love soak in to soften the cold corners of my heart, allowing creative new life to break forth. As a happy fountain leaps jubilantly and tumbles joyfully, come, O Holy Spirit, to transform my melancholy mood until my heart erupts in joy and happiness.

O Father, make my life a melody like that of a great wave, a calm night, a morning sun, a spring rain, a happy fountain! Amen.

Index

◇

369